ONTARIO

TRAVEL GUIDE 2025

Your Ultimate Guide To The Land Of Lakes And Wonders

JIM M. DAVIS

Copyright ©

Disclaimer

This book is intended to serve as a general guide for travel planning. While every effort has been made to provide accurate and up-to-date information, readers should verify details such as business hours, pricing and local regulations before making final travel arrangements. The author and publisher are not liable for any loss, inconvenience or problem that may arise from the use of the information in this manual.

The recommendations and insights presented here are based on research and personal experience. However, this guide should not be considered a substitute for professional advice or guidance from local experts. Travelers are advised to stay informed, respect local customs and laws, and prioritize their safety at all times.

Acknowledgments

Creating this guide has been an enriching experience and I am sincerely grateful to everyone who contributed to its development.

I would like to express my deepest appreciation to the wonderful people of this destination, whose kindness, knowledge and hospitality contributed significantly to the content of this book. Their unique perspectives and stories added depth and authenticity to this guide.

A heartfelt thank you to the many individuals – locals, travelers and industry experts – who shared their

valuable insights and recommendations. Your contributions have helped make this guide a comprehensive and informative resource.
I am also very grateful to my family and friends for their unwavering support, encouragement and patience throughout this project. Her belief in my work was a constant source of motivation.

Finally, I would like to thank you, the reader, for choosing this guide as your travel companion. I hope it serves as a helpful resource and inspires you to embrace new experiences with curiosity and openness.

Table of contents

Introduction

Welcome to the Ontario Travel Guide 2025, your ultimate companion for exploring one of Canada's most diverse and fascinating provinces. Whether you're an adventure seeker, a culture lover or simply looking for a relaxing getaway, Ontario offers an incredible selection of experiences to suit every traveler's desires. From the bustling metropolis of Toronto to the tranquil landscapes of Algonquin Park, the province seamlessly blends urban excitement with natural beauty.

Ontario, the heart of Canada, is a place where contrasts come to life. It is home to the famous Niagara Falls, one of the world's most famous natural wonders, but also offers quiet, picturesque towns that offer a glimpse into the country's rich history and heritage. With over 250,000 lakes, sprawling forests and vibrant cities, Ontario invites travelers to immerse themselves in its breathtaking scenery, diverse cultural offerings and welcoming communities.

In this guide, we take you on a journey through Ontario's must-see destinations, offering practical advice, hidden gems and insider tips to help you experience the province to its fullest. Whether you're planning a quick city trip or an extended cross-region road trip, this travel guide has everything you need to make informed decisions and unforgettable memories.

What makes Ontario so beautiful?

Diverse landscapes: From the breathtaking Great Lakes and rolling vineyards of Niagara to the rugged wilderness of northern Ontario, the province offers landscapes that will captivate any traveler.
World class cities: Experience the multicultural vibrancy of Toronto, the historic charm of Ottawa and the artistic flair of Stratford.
Outdoor Adventures: Ontario is a playground for outdoor enthusiasts, offering hiking, canoeing, skiing and wildlife experiences in its numerous parks and nature reserves.
Rich Culture and Heritage: Discover Indigenous traditions, European influences and modern Canadian culture through Ontario's museums, festivals and local cuisine.
Four Season Destination: Whether you're visiting during the spring blooms, the warmth of summer, the colorful fall foliage or the snowy winter wonderland, Ontario offers attractions and activities year-round.

What to expect from this guide
This guide is intended to be your go-to resource for planning and navigating your trip to Ontario.

Inside you will find:

Practical travel information: From visa requirements to transportation options to ensure a stress-free trip.

Seasonal Travel Advice: Discover the best times to travel and what to expect in each season.

Accommodation Recommendations: Whether you're looking for luxury stays or budget options, we've got you covered.

Must-See Sights: Discover famous landmarks, hidden gems and local favorites that make up Ontario's charm.

Insider Tips and Itineraries: Thoughtful suggestions to help you make the most of your time, whether it's a weekend getaway or a longer exploration.

Cultural Insights: Learn about the province's history, people and customs to enrich your travel experience.

Who is this guide for?

Whether you're looking to explore Ontario's highlights for the first time or you're a seasoned traveler looking for new adventures, this guide is aimed at solo travelers, families, couples and groups alike. Our goal is to provide valuable insights that fit every budget and interest, making it easier for you to plan an unforgettable trip.

Ontario is more than just a destination - it is

Chapter 1:

Welcome to Ontario

Geographical overview: country, climate and natural landscapes

Ontario, Canada's second largest province, has a diverse landscape that offers travelers a mix of natural wonders and vibrant urban centers. Whether you're exploring the rugged wilderness of the north or the bustling cities of the south, Ontario's diverse geography offers something for every traveler.

Geographical diversity

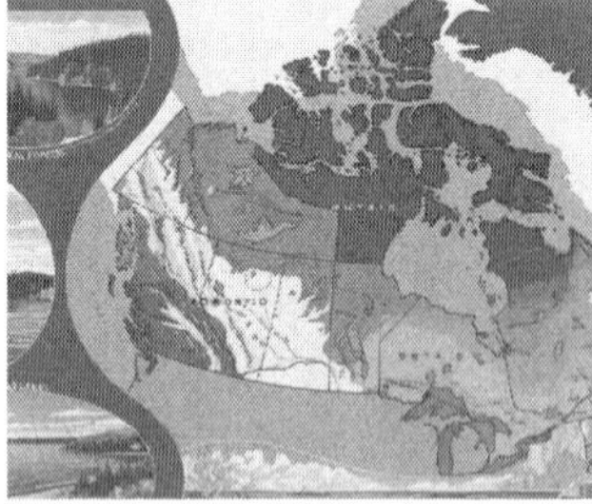

Ontario's landscape is incredibly diverse, ranging from vast northern forests and pristine lakes to dynamic metropolises like Toronto and Ottawa. The province covers over a million square kilometers, making it larger than many other countries.

Key geographical features include:

Forests: Almost 66% of Ontario is covered by forests consisting primarily of spruce, pine and birch, making it a paradise for nature lovers and outdoor adventurers.

Lakes and Rivers: There are approximately 250,000 lakes in Ontario, including the Great Lakes, which contain about a fifth of the world's fresh water.

Urban Centers: Home to major cities such as Toronto, Ottawa and Hamilton, the southern region offers a mix of modern architecture, cultural attractions and vibrant economic activity.

Notable regions

Southern Ontario:
Home to the province's most populous areas, including Toronto and Niagara Falls.
Characterized by rolling farmland, the Great Lakes coastline, and urban development.

Popular for cultural attractions, wine regions and historical landmarks.

Nord-Ontario:
A sparsely populated region known for its rugged wilderness, dense forests and countless lakes.
Perfect for outdoor activities such as camping, fishing and wildlife watching.
Includes the famous Algonquin Provincial Park and the breathtaking landscapes of Lake Superior.

Ontario's Climate and Travel Planning

Ontario has a four-season climate with significant differences between north and south. Understanding seasonal changes will help travelers plan their trips more effectively.

Spring (March - May):
Weather: Cool to mild temperatures (5°C to 15°C), occasional showers.
Ideal for: Sightseeing cities, hiking in provincial parks, and enjoying the blooming cherry blossoms in Toronto's High Park.
Travel Tips: Bring waterproof clothing and layers to adapt to changing temperatures.

Summer (June - August):
Weather: Warm and humid, with temperatures between 20°C and 35°C.
Best for: Exploring the Great Lakes, visiting beaches, attending festivals like the Toronto International Film Festival (TIFF).
Travel Tips: Book your accommodation early as it is peak season and make sure you stay hydrated on hot days.

Autumn (September - November):
Weather: Cool and clear (10°C to 20°C), with stunning fall foliage.
Best for: Scenic countryside road trips, wine tours in Niagara, and hiking in Algonquin Park.

Travel Tips: Pack warm clothing and plan visits to iconic spots like the Niagara Parkway for the best views of fall colors.

Winter (December - February):
Weather: Cold and snowy, with temperatures between -10°C and -30°C in the northern regions.
Ideal for: Blue Mountain skiing, winter festivals and exploring Northern Ontario's frozen landscapes.
Travel Tips: Dress in layers, wear insulated gear, and be prepared for road closures due to snow.

Important Natural Landscapes in Ontario

Ontario is blessed with stunning natural landscapes that attract tourists all year round. The must-visit destinations include:

The Great Lakes

Ontario borders four of the five Great Lakes (Superior, Huron, Erie and Ontario) and offers numerous recreational activities such as boating, swimming and fishing.
Best places: Wasaga Beach (Lake Huron), Sandbanks Provincial Park (Lake Ontario), and Point Pelee National Park (Lake Erie).
Traveler Tip: Visit in the summer for water sports activities or in the fall

for scenic lakeside cruises.

Algonquin Provincial Park

One of Ontario's most famous parks, known for its dense forests, scenic lakes and abundant wildlife.
Activities: Canoeing, camping, hiking and wildlife viewing (moose, beavers and bears).
Travel tip: Book campsites early, especially in summer and fall when the park is busiest.

The Niagara Escarpment

A UNESCO Biosphere Reserve that stretches across Ontario and is home to the famous Niagara Falls and scenic hiking trails.
Best places: Bruce Peninsula National Park, the Cheltenham Badlands and the Niagara Gorge.
Travel Tip: Take the Niagara Parkway for a scenic route filled with wineries, parks and historic sites.

The Thousand Islands

A stunning archipelago of over 1,800 islands along the St. Lawrence River, known for its rich history and scenic boat trips.
Activities: Kayaking, island hopping and exploring Boldt Castle.
Travel Tip: Summer is the best time to visit as various boat tours are available.

Muskoka-Region

A popular escape for cabin dwellers and nature lovers, known for its crystal clear lakes and dense forests.

Activities: Boating, hiking, and visiting charming small towns like Huntsville and Bracebridge.

Travel Tip: Fall is ideal for enjoying the stunning fall foliage and peaceful lakeside retreats.

What to expect in the different regions of Ontario

Nord-Ontario:
Fewer cities, more natural landscapes with breathtaking parks and lakes.
Ideal for adventure seekers seeking canoeing, fishing and remote hiking experiences.
Be prepared for limited cell phone reception and long driving distances between cities.

Southern Ontario:
Densely populated with vibrant cities, cultural attractions and many urban amenities.
Ideal for anyone interested in shopping, entertainment and varied culinary experiences.
The good connection to motorways and public transport makes it easier to explore without a car.

Travel tips for navigating Ontario's geography
Plan accordingly: take travel times into account; Ontario is huge and driving from one region to another can take several hours.

Weather Awareness: Always check the weather forecast before planning outdoor adventures as conditions can change quickly.
Pack Smart: Whether you're exploring the cities or the wilderness, appropriate clothing and equipment is essential.
Respect nature: Follow eco-friendly travel practices and respect the wildlife in Ontario's parks and lakes.

By understanding Ontario's diverse geography, climate and key natural attractions, travelers can better plan their itineraries and enjoy everything the province has to offer. Whether exploring the busy streets of Toronto or the remote wilderness of the north, Ontario promises an unforgettable experience for all types of travelers.

The People and Population: Diversity and Demographics

Ontario is one of the most culturally diverse regions in the world, reflecting a rich diversity of traditions, languages and heritage. With a population of over 15 million people, the province is home to a vibrant mix of cultures, making it a fascinating destination for travelers looking to experience a variety of customs, cuisines and lifestyles. Whether strolling Toronto's multicultural neighborhoods or exploring Indigenous heritage sites, Ontario offers endless opportunities to explore its unique cultural fabric.

Important cultural influences in Ontario

Ontario's cultural identity is shaped by a mix of influences, each contributing to the province's dynamic character. Key cultural influences include:

Indigenous Heritage:

Ontario is home to several indigenous peoples, including the Anishinaabe, Haudenosaunee and Métis, who have inhabited the land for thousands of years.

Indigenous culture is reflected in the province's art, music, storytelling and attractions such as Petroglyphs Provincial Park and the Woodland Cultural Centre.

Traditional practices such as powwows, storytelling circles, and indigenous cuisine (e.g. bannock and venison) continue to thrive and are accessible to visitors.

European influence:

Ontario's European heritage dates primarily to British and French colonization and influenced Ontario's architecture, legal system and language.

Cities like Kingston and Ottawa show strong European influences through their historic buildings like Parliament Hill and Fort Henry.

European settlers also brought with them

agricultural traditions that have developed into Ontario's famous wine regions such as Niagara-on-the-Lake.

Asian communities: Significant waves of immigration from China, India, the Philippines and Pakistan have shaped Ontario's cultural landscape, particularly in urban centers.
The Chinatown neighborhoods in Toronto and Ottawa offer authentic Asian cuisine, bustling markets and traditional festivals such as Chinese New Year and Diwali.
Ontario's culinary scene is enriched with flavors from across Asia, with restaurants serving dim sum, sushi, curries and pho.

Caribbean and African influence: Ontario has a thriving Caribbean and African-Canadian community, particularly in cities like Toronto and Brampton.
Cultural festivals like the Toronto Caribbean Carnival (Caribana) celebrate the vibrant music, dance and food of the Caribbean diaspora.
African markets, music scenes and community centers contribute to the multicultural heartbeat of Ontario's cities.

Multicultural communities in cities
Ontario's urban centers, particularly Toronto and Ottawa, are cultural melting pots where diverse ethnic communities thrive side by side, creating a

unique blend of global traditions and local heritage.

Toronto: The most multicultural city in the world
Toronto is home to over 200 ethnic communities, with more than half of the population born outside Canada.

Neighborhoods to explore:
Chinatown: Experience authentic Chinese cuisine, herbal medicine shops, and lively street festivals.
Little Italy and Little Portugal: Discover European-inspired cafes, trattorias and charming street art.
Greektown: Famous for its annual Taste of the Danforth festival of Greek food and music.
Kensington Market: A bohemian hub with a mix of Latin, Middle Eastern and Caribbean influences.

Ottawa: The Capital of Cultural Harmony
As Canada's capital, Ottawa attracts people from around the world and creates a welcoming, diverse community.
The city is known for its cultural institutions such as the National Gallery of Canada, which showcases indigenous and international art.
Key multicultural events include Winterlude, which celebrates winter traditions from different cultures, and the Ottawa Lebanese Festival.

How Ontario's diversity impacts food,

celebrations and daily life

Ontario's cultural diversity is most evident in:

Kitchen:

Foodies can take a culinary journey around the world without leaving Ontario. The must-try dishes include:

Pea flour and bacon sandwiches (British influence) in Toronto.

Poutine (French-Canadian origin) in Ottawa.

Jamaican patties and roti from Caribbean restaurants in Scarborough.

Authentic sushi and ramen in Markham's Asian food scene.

Food festivals like Taste of the Danforth, the Night Market and the Veg Food Fest showcase international flavors.

Festivals and celebrations:

Ontario hosts a variety of multicultural festivals throughout the year that reflect its diverse heritage. Popular events include:

Toronto International Film Festival (TIFF): Presenting films from around the world.

Caribana: North America's largest Caribbean festival with lively parades and music.

Diwali and Lunar New Year celebrations: Marked with fireworks, traditional performances and delicious cuisine.

National Indigenous Peoples Day: Celebrated with cultural performances, storytelling and craft markets.

Everyday:
Ontario's multiculturalism extends into everyday life, with diverse cultural centers, multilingual signage and inclusive workplaces.
The province embraces cultural fusion, allowing travelers to experience a mix of traditions at local markets, community centers and public art installations.
Multilingual services and guides are available in major tourist areas, making it easier for international travelers to feel at home.

Tips for travelers on how to be respectful of different cultures
Ontario's cultural diversity is one of Ontario's greatest assets, and travelers can enrich their experience by respectfully interacting with diverse communities. Here are some tips for a culturally sensitive visit:

Learn basic greetings:
When visiting ethnic neighborhoods, familiarize yourself with common greetings in languages such as French, Mandarin, or Punjabi.
A simple "Hello" in different languages can create a welcoming connection with locals.

Respect cultural practices:

When visiting religious sites such as temples, mosques, and churches, dress modestly and follow local customs (e.g., taking off shoes, covering shoulders).
Ask before taking photos, especially at ceremonies or at Indigenous heritage sites.

Try new experiences:
Be open to tasting new foods, participate in cultural festivals, and work with local artisans to support community businesses.
Ask questions and show genuine interest in learning about the history of different traditions.

Pay attention to etiquette:
Different cultures have different norms regarding personal space, communication styles and gestures. Observe and adjust accordingly.
Avoid assumptions based on stereotypes and approach interactions with curiosity and respect.

Support local businesses:
Whether you're shopping for souvenirs at Kensington Market or dining in Little India, supporting diverse businesses helps sustain cultural communities.

Ontario's diverse multiculturalism makes it a unique and exciting destination for travelers. Whether you're exploring Toronto's colorful neighborhoods, enjoying international cuisine, or attending cultural festivals, you'll find Ontario's diversity enriching every aspect of your trip. By approaching the multicultural fabric with curiosity and respect, you will gain a deeper understanding of the province and the many cultures that call it home.

Culture and Heritage: Indigenous Roots and Modern Influences

A rich mix of Indigenous traditions and modern influences, Ontario's cultural landscape offers travelers a unique opportunity to explore the province's deep-rooted heritage alongside its modern lifestyle. From ancient rock-cut petroglyphs to thriving Indigenous art communities and multicultural urban landscapes, Ontario offers a fascinating mix of old and new.

Indigenous Cultures and Traditions in Ontario

Ontario is home to a diverse indigenous population, including the Anishinaabe (Ojibwe, Odawa and Potawatomi), Haudenosaunee (Iroquois Confederacy), Cree and Métis. These communities have lived in the region for thousands of years and maintain rich cultural traditions that continue to shape the province today.

Key aspects of Indigenous culture in Ontario:

Language and storytelling:

Indigenous languages such as Ojibwe, Mohawk and Cree are still spoken and preserved through storytelling, an integral part of Indigenous culture. Visitors can experience these oral histories through tours and cultural exhibitions.

Arts and crafts:
Indigenous art in Ontario includes intricate beadwork, quill work and carving, with modern Indigenous artists incorporating traditional themes into contemporary works.
Galleries like the Woodland Cultural Center showcase the development of Indigenous art.

Spiritual practices and ceremonies:
Sacred ceremonies such as smudging, drum circles and powwows are important aspects of Indigenous spirituality and focus on a deep connection to nature and ancestors.

Traditional foods:
Indigenous cuisine includes dishes such as bannock (a type of fried bread), wild rice, venison and fish, often prepared using traditional, environmentally friendly methods.

Connection to the country:
Indigenous peoples have a deep connection to the land, which is reflected in their sustainable practices, including traditional hunting, fishing and farming techniques that have been passed down through generations.

Important cultural landmarks in Ontario

Ontario offers several cultural landmarks where travelers can explore and appreciate the history of indigenous peoples and their contributions to Canadian society. Must-visit websites include:

Woodland Cultural Center (Brantford):
Located on the site of the former Mohawk Institute Residential School, this center preserves and promotes Indigenous culture, art and history.
Visitors can explore exhibits on residential schools, indigenous traditions and contemporary cultural expressions.
Tip: Take guided tours to gain a deeper insight into the heritage of Ontario's indigenous peoples.

Petroglyphs Provincial Park (Kawartha Lakes):
Home to the largest collection of Indigenous rock carvings (petroglyphs) in Canada, dating back over 1,000 years.
These carvings depict turtles, snakes and other spiritual symbols that hold great meaning in Anishinaabe culture.
Tip: Visit the park's visitor center to learn more about the spiritual meaning of the carvings and their connection to Indigenous cosmology.

Manitoulin Island:
The world's largest freshwater island is rich in indigenous culture and home to several First Nations communities such as the Ojibwe of Wikwemikong.
Travelers can experience powwows, canoe tours with indigenous guides, and traditional craft workshops.

Tip: Attend the annual meeting Wiikwemkoong Cultural festival to experience authentic indigenous music and dance.

Six Nations of the Grand River (near Brantford):
The largest First Nations reserve in Canada offers cultural experiences, craft markets and historic sites like Chiefswood National Historic Site.

Tip: Explore Her Majesty's Mohawk Royal Chapel, one of the oldest surviving chapels associated with the Haudenosaunee.

Indigenous experiences in Ottawa:
The capital offers cultural programs, including Mādahòkì Farm, where visitors can take part in traditional activities such as storytelling and festivals featuring indigenous cuisine.

How to Responsibly Experience Ontario's Indigenous Heritage
When exploring Ontario's Indigenous sites and traditions, respect for Indigenous culture and heritage is critical. Here are some guidelines for responsible travel:

Find out before you go:
Learn about the history and customs of the indigenous communities you plan to visit.
Read more about the Truth and Reconciliation Commission of Canada to better understand the historical and cultural context.

Look for authentic experiences:
Support Indigenous businesses such as art galleries, tours and restaurants that provide authentic experiences and benefit local communities.
Look for Indigenous tourism initiatives like Indigenous Tourism Ontario (ITO) that promote responsible travel.

Respect cultural protocols:
Always ask permission before photographing people or sacred sites.
Follow guidelines at cultural monuments to avoid disturbing cultural artifacts or sacred areas.

Interact with Locals:
Attend cultural events, workshops and storytelling sessions to gain first-hand insights from Indigenous leaders and elders.
Show respect by listening carefully and participating with an open mind.

Support sustainable practices:
Choose eco-friendly travel options and respect the environment by following Leave No Trace principles when visiting natural sites of cultural significance.

Modern cultural influences shape Ontario today
While Ontario's Indigenous heritage remains a cornerstone of its cultural identity, modern influences have transformed the province into a vibrant, multicultural hub.

Multiculturalism:
Ontario's cities, particularly Toronto and Ottawa, are known for their cultural diversity, incorporating influences from around the world in areas such as food, arts and entertainment.
Annual festivals such as the Toronto International Film Festival (TIFF) and Ottawa's Winterlude celebrate the province's global connections.

Urban lifestyle and innovation:
Ontario's modern lifestyle is characterized by cutting-edge technology, a thriving arts scene and an active outdoor culture.
Cities like Toronto offer a dynamic mix of skyscrapers, international cuisine and cultural districts, while smaller cities preserve Ontario's rich heritage with a modern twist.

Fusion cuisine:
Ontario's modern cuisine combines elements of its indigenous roots and international influences. Chefs create fusion dishes like bison tacos, butter tarts with indigenous flavors and sushi-inspired creations using local fish.

Music and entertainment:
Ontario's music scene reflects a mix of Indigenous, classical, rock and hip-hop influences, with artists such as Drake, The Tragically Hip and Indigenous musicians

such as Jeremy Dutcher making their mark across the globe.

Sports and leisure:
Traditional Indigenous sports such as lacrosse, which originated with the Iroquois, have influenced Ontario's sporting culture, alongside popular games such as hockey and basketball.

Ontario's culture and heritage offer travelers an enriching experience where ancient traditions meet modern influences in a seamless blend. Whether exploring sacred Indigenous sites, attending cultural festivals or enjoying modern city life, Ontario presents a dynamic and respectful celebration of its diverse heritage. By engaging responsibly and leveraging the province's cultural wealth, travelers can develop a deeper appreciation for Ontario's past, present and future.

Chapter 2:

Basic travel information

Time Zone and Currency: Practical Basics

When planning a trip to Ontario, be sure to know the time zone and currency to ensure a smooth and hassle-free experience. In this section you'll find practical information about Ontario's time zones and currencies, as well as financial tips to help travelers manage their expenses effectively.

Ontario time zone

Ontario falls into two time zones that travelers should be aware of to avoid confusion when planning itineraries or making reservations:

Eastern Time Zone (ET):
Covers most of Ontario, including major cities such as Toronto, Ottawa, Niagara Falls and Kingston.

Standard time: UTC -5 hours
Daylight Saving Time (DST): Observed from the second Sunday in March to the first Sunday in November and advances clocks by one hour to UTC -4 hours.

Central Time Zone (CT):
Applies to parts of northwestern Ontario, including cities such as Kenora, Dryden and parts of the Thunder Bay District.

Standard time: UTC -6 hours

Daylight Saving Time (DST): Observed similarly to Eastern Time, with clocks set forward to UTC -5 hours.

Impact on travelers:

Travelers from different time zones should prepare for possible jet lag and adjust their schedules accordingly.

It's helpful to set devices to Ontario time upon arrival to stay on top of planned activities.

Public services, attractions and shops typically operate on Eastern Time, so travelers should be aware of time differences when visiting the western part of the province.

Pro tip: Use mobile apps like World Clock (iOS/Android) to keep track of Ontario's time relative to your home country.

Currency in Ontario

The official currency in Ontario is the Canadian Dollar (CAD), symbolized by $ or C$, and is available in the following denominations:

Banknotes: $5, $10, $20, $50 and $100

Coins: 5 cents (Nickel), 10 cents (Dime), 25 cents (Quarter), $1 (Loonie) and $2 (Toonie)

Exchange rates and options:

Exchange rates for CAD fluctuate daily, so it is advisable to check current exchange rates before transacting. Currency exchange options include:

The bank:

Major banks such as RBC (Royal Bank of Canada), TD Canada Trust and Scotiabank offer competitive exchange rates and currency exchange services.
Most banks are open Monday to Friday from 9:00 a.m. to 5:00 p.m., with limited opening hours on weekends.

Cash change machines:

You can find them in airports, shopping centers and popular tourist areas, but they may charge higher fees than banks.

ATMs:

Widely used throughout Ontario and provides convenient access to Canadian dollars.
Fees may apply for withdrawals. Travelers should therefore check with their home bank about the fees for international withdrawals.

Online exchange services:

Platforms like Wise (formerly TransferWise), Revolut or PayPal offer good exchange rates with minimal fees for digital transactions.

Recommended budgeting apps:

To track expenses and manage finances effectively, travelers can use budgeting apps like:
XE Currency Converter – To check real-time exchange rates.
Mint – Helps monitor expenses in CAD.
Splitwise – Useful for splitting travel expenses into groups.

Pro tip: Always carry a small amount of local currency with you for smaller expenses like tips, vending machines, or public transportation fares.

Cash vs. Card: What Travelers Should Know

Ontario is a predominantly cashless society, with most businesses and establishments accepting credit and debit cards. However, cash is still useful in certain situations.

Using Credit and Debit Cards:

Widely used in hotels, restaurants, tourist attractions and shops.

Contactless payments (tap-to-pay) are common, with most terminals supporting Visa, Mastercard and American Express.

Some companies may charge an international transaction fee, so it is advisable to check with your card provider.

Mobile payments:

Digital wallets such as Apple Pay, Google Pay and Samsung Pay are becoming increasingly popular in Ontario, allowing travelers to make secure, contactless payments.

Where cash may be needed:

Small Towns and Rural Areas – Some local businesses or farmers markets may prefer cash payments.

Tips and gratuities – While tipping is common in Ontario, some service providers may prefer cash for convenience.

Public Transportation – Some transit systems, particularly in smaller cities, may only accept exact change when purchasing tickets on board.

ATM Availability:
ATMs are easily accessible in urban centers, airports and shopping areas. Popular ATM networks include:
Interac (Canada's main debit network)
Plus and Cirrus (international networks) for foreign bank cards

Pro Tip: For security reasons, choose ATMs in banks or reputable stores and avoid isolated machines in remote areas.

Travel Budgeting Tips for Ontario
To make the most of your trip without overspending, consider the following tips:
Plan a daily budget:
Average costs in Ontario:
Meals: CAD 15-40 per person
Public transportation: CAD 3-10 per trip
Attractions: CAD 20-50 per ticket
Adjust your budget to suit your travel style, whether luxury or budget.
Use prepaid travel cards:
Preloaded with CAD, it offers better exchange rates and security over carrying large amounts of cash.
Look for discounts:
Many attractions offer discounted rates for students, seniors and families.

Consider purchasing a CityPASS to receive pooled savings on major attractions.

Avoid dynamic currency conversions:

When using your card, always choose to bill in CAD rather than your home currency to avoid unfavorable conversion rates.

Emergency fund:

Have a cash reserve on hand for emergencies such as unexpected travel delays or service interruptions.

Understanding Ontario's time zone differences and financial landscape will help travelers plan their itinerary and budget more effectively. While Ontario is largely cashless, a mix of payment methods ensure seamless transactions during your trip. Staying informed about exchange rates, budgeting tools, and spending habits will improve your travel experience and avoid unexpected financial surprises.

Visa requirements and border entry: What you need to know

As part of Canada, Ontario has specific visa and entry requirements that travelers must follow to ensure a smooth journey. Whether you are traveling by air, land or sea, it is important to be aware of visa requirements, border crossing procedures and customs regulations to avoid unnecessary delays.

Visa requirements for international visitors

Canada offers different visa and entry options depending on nationality, purpose of visit and length of stay. Travelers should clarify their eligibility and submit an application well in advance of their trip.

Besuchervisum (Temporary Resident Visa – TRV)

Required for nationals of countries that are not eligible for visa-free entry to Canada.
Valid for stays of up to 6 months (unless otherwise stated by immigration officials).

The application process includes:

1. Complete an online form via the Immigration, Refugees and Citizenship Canada (IRCC) website.
2. Providing supporting documents such as proof of financial support, itinerary and accommodation details.
3. Payment of a processing fee (approximately CAD$100).

Biometrics (fingerprints and photos) may be required.
Pro tip: Apply for a visa at least 8 weeks before your travel date to allow for processing time.

Electronic Travel Authorization (eTA)

Applies to travelers from visa-free countries (e.g. USA, UK, Australia, EU countries) entering by plane.
Electronically linked to the passport and valid for up to 5 years or until the passport expires.

Cost: $7 CAD. Approval is usually instant but can take up to 72 hours.
Travelers must submit their application through the official Government of Canada website.
Important: An eTA is NOT required to enter Canada by land or sea.

Travelers who are exempt from visa requirements
United States citizens do not need a visa or eTA to enter Canada.
A valid passport or approved travel document must be presented at the border.

Work and study permit
Visitors wishing to work or study in Ontario must apply for the appropriate permit prior to arrival.
Short-term studies (less than 6 months) can be carried out with a visitor visa, while longer courses require a study permit.
Pro tip: Always check the official Canadian government websites for the latest visa requirements before traveling.

Crossing the US-Canada border by car or plane
Ontario shares a long border with the United States and travelers can enter via various land crossings or by air. Knowing the requirements in advance can make border crossings smoother and more efficient.

Entry by plane

When travelers fly into Ontario from the United States or other international locations, they must go through Canadian border security checks upon arrival at airports such as the following:
Toronto Pearson International Airport (YYZ)
Ottawa Macdonald-Cartier International Airport (YOW)
Billy Bishop Toronto City Airport (YTZ)
Required documents for air travelers:
A valid passport (must be valid for at least 6 months from the date of entry).

Valid visa or eTA (if required).
Return flight ticket and proof of sufficient funds for the stay.
Customs declaration: Travelers must complete a Canada Border Services Agency (CBSA) declaration card either electronically or on paper before immigration control.

Entry by car (land border crossings)
Travelers entering Ontario from the United States may use one of the many land border crossings, including:
Grenze Windsor-Detroit (Ambassador Bridge, Detroit-Windsor-Tunnel)
Niagara Falls border (Rainbow Bridge, Peace Bridge, Lewiston-Queenston Bridge)
Thousand Islands Border Crossing (near Kingston, ON)

Requirements for crossing by car:
A valid passport or an approved travel document such as: B. a NEXUS card (for accelerated processing).

Proof of automobile insurance that covers driving in Canada.

Vehicle documents.

Pro Tip: Expect delays during rush hours and major holidays. Use online wait time tools at the border to plan.

Important points to keep in mind when crossing the border:

Be prepared to answer questions about the purpose of your visit and length of stay.

Travelers may be asked to provide proof of a hotel reservation and sufficient funds.

When traveling with minors, parental consent may be required if one parent is not present.

Customs regulations: What you can and cannot bring into Ontario

The Canada Border Services Agency (CBSA) enforces strict regulations on what items travelers can bring into Ontario. To avoid penalties, it is important to follow these guidelines:

Eligible items (with restrictions)

Personal Items: Clothing, personal electronics, and travel essentials for personal use.

Alcohol:

Visitors of legal drinking age (19 in Ontario) may bring:

Up to 1.5 liters of wine or

1.14 liters of spirits or
8.5 liters of beer.
Amounts that exceed these limits are subject to duties and taxes.

Plate:

Up to 200 cigarettes, 50 cigars and 200 grams of tobacco.

Currency:

Travelers can bring any amount of money with them, but amounts over $10,000 CAD must be declared at the border.

Prohibited and Restricted Items

Fresh fruits and vegetables: Some agricultural products are subject to restrictions to prevent the spread of pests.
Meat and Dairy: Strict restrictions apply; Check the latest import regulations before bringing food with you.
Firearms and Weapons: Generally prohibited except for hunting purposes with prior authorization.
Cannabis: Although legal in Canada, transporting cannabis across international borders is illegal.

Duty-free allowance for returning visitors

Visitors leaving Ontario and returning to their home country may be eligible for tax refunds on certain purchases. Check with CBSA and your home country's customs authorities for duty allowances.
Pro Tip: To avoid delays, declare all items honestly and keep receipts for valuable goods.

Travel tips for a smooth entry

What you need to know before you go:
Visit the official CBSA website for the latest border guidelines and wait times.
Have documentation ready:
Keep your passport, visa and other travel documents easily accessible.
Declare all goods:
Items purchased duty-free should also be declared to avoid penalties.
Use Trusted Traveler programs:
Consider enrolling in programs like NEXUS to expedite border clearance if you frequently travel between the U.S. and Canada.
Check for COVID-19 or health restrictions:
Before you leave, make sure you meet any vaccination or health screening requirements.

When travelers understand Ontario's visa requirements, border entry processes and customs regulations, they can enjoy a smooth and stress-free trip. Whether you arrive by plane or by road, being prepared with the correct documentation and import requirements can help you avoid unexpected problems at the border.

Language and communication: English, French and local expressions

Ontario is a linguistically diverse province, with English and French as official languages, as well as a variety of other languages spoken due to its multicultural population. Understanding the linguistic landscape and knowing a few key phrases can greatly improve a traveler's experience, making it easier to navigate and engage with locals.

Major languages spoken in Ontario

English (main language):
English is the predominant language throughout Ontario, particularly in urban centers such as Toronto, Ottawa and Hamilton.
Most services, including transportation, hospitality and tourism, are provided primarily in English.

French (second official language):
French is commonly spoken in certain regions, particularly in eastern Ontario (e.g. Ottawa, Cornwall) and parts of northern Ontario (e.g. Sudbury).
Ontario has the largest French-speaking population outside of Quebec and travelers can find bilingual services in many government offices and tourist attractions.

Other commonly spoken languages:
Due to Ontario's cultural diversity, travelers may hear a variety of languages spoken, including:
Mandarin and Cantonese: Predominantly in Toronto and Markham, home to large Chinese communities.

Punjabi, Hindi and Urdu: Common in South Asian communities in cities such as Brampton and Mississauga.
Italian and Portuguese: Spoken in neighborhoods with European heritage, such as Little Italy and Little Portugal in Toronto.
Indigenous languages: In certain areas, particularly northern Ontario, there are indigenous languages such as Ojibwe and Cree.
Pro Tip: In major tourist areas, signage and public announcements are often available in both English and French.

Useful phrases and tips for communication
Even if travelers are fluent in English, it can be helpful to understand some French expressions or local slang, especially in bilingual regions. Here are a few useful phrases:

Common English expressions for travelers:
Hello: Hello / Hello
Thank you: thank you / thank you
Apologies: Sorry/Excuse me
How much does it cost? - How much does that cost?
Where is...? - Where can I find...?
Can you help me? - Could you please help me?

Common French expressions travelers might encounter:
Bonjour (bohn-zhoor) – Hello / Good day
Merci (see more) – Thank you

Do you speak English? (par-lay voo ahn-glay?) – Do you speak English?
How much does it cost? (kohm-byen saw koot?) – How much does it cost?
West...? (ooh?) – Where is...?
I don't understand (zhuh nuh kohm-prahn pah) - I don't understand

Canadian English and Slang you should know:
Ontario residents may use informal slang or expressions unique to Canada, such as:
"Eh" – A friendly way to ask for approval or affirmation (e.g. "Nice day, huh?")
"Double-double" – A coffee with two types of cream and two types of sugar, commonly ordered at Tim Hortons.
"Toque" (pronounced "tuke") – A knitted winter hat.
"Loonie" and "Toonie" – Slang for the Canadian $1 and $2 coins.
Pro tip: If you ask for directions, locals are generally friendly and helpful, but speaking clearly and slowly can help with effective communication.

Recommended language apps for non-English speakers
For travelers who are not fluent in English or French, technology can be a helpful tool. The following language apps can help with translation and communication:

Google Translate (Free | iOS & Android)
Supports translation of text, voice and even signage via camera.

Offline mode available for situations without internet access.

Duolingo (Free with paid options | iOS & Android)
Offers basic English and French learning courses tailored to travelers.
Playful lessons make language learning fun and interactive.

iTranslate (Free with Premium Features | iOS & Android)
Provides real-time voice translation for conversations.
Works well for translating menus and signs.

SayHi Translate (Free | iOS & Android)
Focuses on voice-to-text translation, ideal for real-time interactions.
Ideal for communication in restaurants and taxis.

TripLingo (Paid | iOS & Android)
In addition to translation functions, it also offers cultural insights.
Includes emergency phrases and etiquette tips for different countries.
Pro tip: Download voice apps before you arrive in Ontario and use offline features to avoid roaming charges.

Travel tips for effective communication

Speak slowly and clearly: Not everyone is fluent in English, especially in rural areas.
Learn basic French greetings: This can make interaction easier in Francophone areas.
Use hand gestures and visual aids: Pointing to maps or using pictures can help overcome language barriers.
Carry a translation card with you: Write down important phrases or questions about accommodations, transportation, and dietary restrictions.
Look for official bilingual signs: many government agencies, airports and tourist destinations offer services in both languages.

Understanding Ontario's linguistic landscape can greatly improve your travel experience and make interactions smoother and more enjoyable. Although English is widely spoken, a few French phrases and the use of language apps can be invaluable. Whether exploring bustling cities or rural areas, understanding language nuances and cultural diversity will help travelers navigate Ontario with ease.

Chapter 3:

When to Visit Ontario

Best seasons to travel: weather and activities

Ontario offers a unique experience in every season and is an attractive destination all year round. Whether you're looking for winter adventures, vibrant fall colors, spring blooms or summer festivals, Ontario's diverse landscape and climate offers something for every traveler. Understanding the pros and cons of each season can help plan the perfect visit.

Spring (March to May)

Spring in Ontario brings mild temperatures and blooming landscapes, making it an excellent time for outdoor exploration before the summer crowds arrive.

Advantages:

Milder temperatures, ideal for sightseeing and outdoor activities.

Beautiful cherry blossoms in cities like Toronto and High Park.

Lower accommodation prices compared to summer.

Maple syrup festivals in rural areas, such as Muskoka and the Kawarthas.

Disadvantages:

Unpredictable weather with occasional rain and persistent winter cold.

Some seasonal attractions may remain closed until late spring.

Best Activities:

Hiking: Explore the trails in Algonquin Park and Bruce Peninsula National Park that come alive with spring flora.

Wildlife Viewing: Visit wildlife refuges like Point Pelee National Park to spot birds during migration season.

Festivals: Enjoy events like the Canadian Tulip Festival in Ottawa.

City Tours: Explore Toronto, Ottawa and Niagara Falls with fewer crowds and pleasant weather.

Pro tip: Pack layers and waterproof gear as spring weather can be unpredictable.

Summer (June to August)

Summer is the peak travel season in Ontario, offering warm weather and tons of outdoor activities.

Advantages:

Long daylight hours, perfect for sightseeing and outdoor adventures.

Festivals and events are in full swing across the province.

Beach destinations like Wasaga Beach and Sandbanks Provincial Park are at their best.

Disadvantages:

Higher prices for accommodation and flights due to peak demand.

Popular attractions like Niagara Falls can be crowded.

Humid conditions, particularly in southern Ontario.

Best Activities:

Outdoor Adventure: Canoeing and kayaking in the Muskoka Lakes region.
National and Provincial Parks: Camping, hiking and wildlife viewing in parks like Killarney and Algonquin.
Urban Exploration: Experience bustling cities with lively courtyards, cultural festivals and night markets.
Water Activities: Enjoy boating on the Great Lakes and refreshing yourself on freshwater beaches.
Pro tip: Book accommodations and tickets in advance to avoid peak season price increases and ensure availability.

Autumn (September to November)
Fall is one of the most picturesque seasons in Ontario, with colorful foliage and pleasant temperatures.

Advantages:
Stunning fall colors, especially in regions like Algonquin Park and the Niagara Escarpment.
Less crowds compared to summer.
Mild temperatures ideal for hiking and outdoor excursions.
Wine tours and Thanksgiving festivals in areas like Niagara-on-the-Lake.
Disadvantages:
Cooler temperatures in late fall, particularly in northern Ontario.
Some summer attractions begin to close after September.

Best Activities:

Leaf Peeping: Drive along scenic routes like the Muskoka Lakes or the Bruce Peninsula.
Hiking: Hiking trails in Rouge National Urban Park and Dundas Peak offer breathtaking views.
Food and Wine Experiences: Attend grape harvest festivals and sample fresh produce at farmers markets.
Cultural Events: Enjoy art exhibitions and theater performances in major cities.
Pro tip: Plan visits between mid-September and early October to enjoy the brightest fall colors.

Winter (December to February)

Winter in Ontario offers a true winter wonderland experience with plenty of opportunities for snow sports and holidays.

Advantages:

Picturesque snow-covered landscapes ideal for winter photography.
Exciting winter sports such as skiing, snowboarding and ice skating.
Festive holiday events and Christmas markets, particularly in Toronto and Ottawa.
Lower travel costs for off-peak areas (excluding ski resorts).

Disadvantages:

Harsh temperatures, especially in northern Ontario.
Due to heavy snowfall, some outdoor attractions may be closed.
Driving conditions may be difficult due to snow and ice.

Best Activities:

Winter Sports: Skiing at Blue Mountain or dog sledding in Algonquin Park.
Ice Skating: Enjoy famous outdoor ice rinks like Nathan Phillips Square in Toronto or Rideau Canal in Ottawa.
Festivals: Experience the Winterlude Festival in Ottawa or the Winter Festival of Lights in Niagara Falls.
Cozy Indoor Attractions: Visit museums and art galleries and enjoy Ontario's thriving café culture.
Pro tip: Dress in layers and wear thermal clothing to stay comfortable in freezing temperatures.

Peak tourist season and how to avoid crowds

High season (June to August):
Expect large crowds at major attractions such as Niagara Falls, the CN Tower and popular national parks.
To avoid crowds, visit the sites early in the morning or on weekdays.

Low season (April-May, September-October):
These months offer a balance between good weather and fewer crowds, making them ideal for budget-conscious travelers.

Low season (November-March):
While some attractions may be closed, it's a great time for winter sports enthusiasts and those looking for lower travel costs.
Pro tip: Consider visiting smaller towns and lesser-known parks to avoid peak season traffic and discover hidden gems.

Ontario offers a range of experiences in every season, catering to nature lovers, adventure seekers and culture enthusiasts alike. Whether you're drawn to the vibrant colors of fall, the snowy winter landscapes, the festivals of summer, or the blooming beauty of spring, planning your trip around seasonal highlights will help you make the most of your visit.

Festivals and events: From the winter carnival to the summer festival

Ontario is a hub of vibrant festivals and events celebrating its rich cultural diversity, artistic heritage and seasonal beauty. From world-famous international gatherings to enchanting local festivals, there's always something going on in the province. Whether you're interested in film, food, music or cultural celebrations, planning your visit around these events can enrich your Ontario experience.

The best annual festivals to plan

If you're visiting Ontario, these major annual festivals should be on your radar. They attract thousands of visitors and offer unforgettable experiences:

Toronto International Film Festival (TIFF)
When: September
Wo: Toronto

Why go: One of the world's most prestigious film festivals, TIFF showcases hundreds of films from around the world and features screenings, celebrity viewings and panel discussions.
Travel Tip: Book tickets and accommodation months in advance as the city fills up quickly during the festival.

Winterlude
When: February
Where: Ottawa
Why go: A celebration of winter with ice sculpting competitions, skating on the Rideau Canal (the world's longest ice rink), and various snow-themed activities.
Travel tip: Dress warmly and stay overnight in downtown Ottawa for easy access to festival venues.

Caribana (Caribbean Carnival in Toronto)
When: End of July to beginning of August
Wo: Toronto
Why go: North America's largest Caribbean festival features lively parades, lavish costumes, music and food that celebrate Caribbean culture and heritage.
Travel Tip: Arrive early to get a good viewing spot for the Grand Parade and explore smaller events leading up to the main event.

Canadian National Exhibition (CNE)
When: End of August to beginning of September
Wo: Toronto

Why go: A family-friendly event with rides, live entertainment, unique food vendors and exhibits from technology to agriculture.
Travel tip: Consider purchasing an all-day ticket to get the most out of the exhibition grounds.

Niagara-Eisweinfestival
When: January
Where: Niagara-Region
Why go: Celebrate Ontario's famous ice wine with tastings, vineyard tours and gourmet dining pairings in one of Canada's most renowned wine regions.
Travel Tip: Dress warmly and take advantage of the wine tour packages that include transportation.

Stratford-Festival
When: April to October
Wo: Stratford
Why Go: A world-famous theater festival featuring exceptional productions of Shakespeare plays and contemporary works.
Travel Tip: Plan to stay overnight to enjoy both the matinee and evening performances.

Ottawa Tulip Festival
When: May
Where: Ottawa
Why go: Thousands of colorful tulips bloom throughout the city, symbolizing the long-standing friendship between Canada and the Netherlands.

Travel tip: Take a boat trip along the Rideau Canal and enjoy a unique view of the tulips.

Lesser known local events for unique cultural experiences

While large festivals attract global attention, Ontario's smaller events offer authentic experiences that highlight the province's local culture and charm:

Elmira Maple Syrup Festival

When: April

Where: Elmira (near Waterloo)

Why go: A small-town celebration of Canada's legendary maple syrup with pancake breakfasts, syrup tastings and local crafts.

Travel Tip: Arrive early to enjoy the freshest maple snacks and avoid long lines.

Muskoka Cranberry Festival

When: October

Wo: Bala (Muskoka)

Why go: Celebrate Ontario's cranberry harvest with farm tours, tastings and scenic tours of the cranberry swamps.

Travel Tip: Try the locally made cranberry wine and desserts.

Kitchener-Waterloo Oktoberfest

When: October

Wo: Kitchener-Waterloo

Why go: North America's largest Oktoberfest features Bavarian-style beer gardens, traditional music and authentic German cuisine.
Travel Tip: Book a ticket to the Oktoberfest Gala for a premium experience.

Sound of Music Festival
When: June
Wo: Burlington
Why go: A free outdoor music festival with a diverse lineup of rock, pop and indie artists right on Lake Ontario.
Travel Tip: Bring a blanket and arrive early to secure a good spot for the main stage performances.

Sudbury Blueberry Festival
When: July
Wo: Sudbury
Why go: A week-long celebration of the region's famous wild blueberries with food tastings, family-friendly activities and live music.
Travel Tip: Don't miss the blueberry pancakes at local breakfast spots during the festival.

Collingwood Elvis Festival
When: July
Wo: Collingwood
Why Go: A whimsical tribute to Elvis Presley with tribute artists, competitions and themed events.
Travel tip: Book your accommodation early as this small town gets busy over the festival weekend.

Tips for booking accommodation during festival season
Attending Ontario's popular festivals requires careful planning, especially when it comes to securing accommodation. Here are some useful tips:

Book early: Many hotels and holiday apartments are fully booked months in advance for major festivals such as TIFF and Caribana. Booking 3-6 months in advance will give you better prices and options.

Consider alternative stays: If hotels are fully booked, look for vacation rentals, hostels, or even homestays through platforms like Airbnb and Vrbo.

Staying outside the city center: For large events in Toronto and Ottawa, consider staying in nearby suburbs with access to public transportation to save costs.

Use festival packages: Some events offer bundled travel packages that include accommodation, tickets and tours – saving both money and planning effort.

Transport schedule: During large festivals, public transport may be the best option to avoid traffic jams and expensive parking fees.

Check the cancellation policy: Flexible bookings can be beneficial if your plans change or festival dates are postponed.

Pro tip: Download festival apps (if available) to stay up to date on event schedules, venue changes and special offers.

Ontario's festivals and events showcase the province's cultural richness and dynamic spirit, offering something for every traveler. Whether you want to experience the world-famous energy of Caribana or discover the enchanting traditions of a small-town festival, planning your trip around these events will make your trip even more memorable.

Chapter 4:

Prepare for your trip

Packaging for Ontario's diverse climate

Packing for a trip to Ontario requires careful planning as the province experiences varying weather conditions and offers a wide range of activities. Whether you're exploring bustling cities, hiking through national parks, or taking a scenic road trip, having the right items will ensure a smooth and enjoyable journey.

Clothing recommendations for every season

Ontario's climate varies significantly throughout the year, so it's important to pack according to the season.

Spring (March – May)

Weather: Mild to cool, with occasional rain. Temperatures range from 5°C to 15°C (41°F to 59°F).

What to pack:

Light jacket or raincoat
Layered clothing (sweaters, long-sleeved shirts)
Waterproof shoes or boots
Umbrella or compact rain poncho
Sunglasses and sunscreen for sunny days

Summer (June – August)

Weather: Warm to hot, with temperatures between 20°C and 30°C (68°F to 86°F). Humidity can be high in southern Ontario.

What to pack:
Lightweight, breathable clothing (cotton T-shirts, shorts, dresses)
Sun hat and sunglasses
Swimsuit for beaches and lakes
Comfortable hiking shoes or sandals
Insect spray (especially for outdoor activities)
Reusable water bottle to stay hydrated

Autumn (September – November)
Weather: Cool and clear, with bright autumn leaves. Temperatures range from 10°C to 20°C (50°F to 68°F).

What to pack:
Warm sweaters and layers
Light but warm jacket
Scarf and gloves for late autumn excursions
Comfortable hiking shoes for exploring parks
Camera to capture the stunning fall colors

Winter (December – February)
Weather: Cold, snowy and icy, with temperatures between -10°C and -30°C (14°F to -22°F). Wind chill can make it feel colder.

What to pack:
Heavy winter coat (preferably insulated)

Thermal layers (wool socks, thermal underwear)
Waterproof boots with good grip
Hat, gloves and scarf
Lip balm and moisturizer to combat dry air
Hand warmer for extra warmth

Must-have item for urban and outdoor adventures

Ontario offers both bustling city experiences and nature escapes. Tailor your packing list to your activities:

Urban Adventures (Toronto, Ottawa, Niagara Falls, etc.)

Comfortable hiking shoes for exploring the city
Casual yet stylish clothing for dining out
Portable phone charger
Public transportation map or app (e.g. Toronto PRESTO map)
Small daypack for carrying the essentials
Camera for city views and sights
Travel guides or digital travel apps

Outdoor Adventures (Algonquin Park, Bruce Peninsula, Muskoka, etc.)

Waterproof hiking shoes
Weather-appropriate outdoor clothing
Lightweight backpack for day hikes
Reusable water bottle and energy snacks
First aid kit and bug spray
Map or GPS device for remote areas
Flashlight or headlamp for camping trips

Pro tip: Always check the weather forecast before your trip to adjust your packing list accordingly.

Packing checklist for different travel purposes

To make your travel preparation easier, use the following checklists depending on your travel style:

Checklist for hikes and nature trips:

Hiking boots/shoes
Moisture-wicking clothing
Rain jacket and extra layers
Hat and sunglasses
Snacks and hydration pack
Compass or GPS device
Wildlife guide or binoculars

Checklist for exploring the city:

Comfortable hiking shoes
Casual outfits for the day
More elegant outfit for evening outings
Portable umbrella
Local maps or city guide app
Reusable shopping bag for souvenirs

Roadtrip-Checkliste:

Driving license and rental car documents
Road map or GPS navigation app
Roadside emergency kit (jumper cables, flashlight)
Snacks and drinks for long journeys
Comfortable travel pillow
Music playlist or audio books

Reusable travel mugs and utensils

Checklist for winter sports and skiing:
Ski/snowboard equipment (if not rented)
Insulated, waterproof clothing
Thick socks and thermal layers
Ski goggles and helmet
Lip balm and sunscreen (against snow glare)
Energy snacks and hydration

Additional packing tips

Pack light, pack smart: Use packing cubes to organize clothes and maximize suitcase space.
Multifunctional items: Choose clothes that can be combined for different occasions.
Check travel restrictions: Make sure items such as liquids meet airline regulations.
Prepare for emergencies: Have a small first aid kit with the most important medications and bandages ready.
Travel documents: Always carry copies of your passport, insurance and booking confirmations with you.

Packing for Ontario requires a strategic approach based on the season and planned activities. Whether you're exploring the bustling streets of Toronto or venturing into the vast provincial wilderness, having the right essentials will ensure a comfortable and enjoyable journey. Plan wisely and enjoy everything Ontario has to offer!

Health and safety tips for urban and outdoor adventures

For a stress-free experience, a safe and healthy trip to Ontario is essential. The province offers high standards of health, reliable emergency services and a generally safe environment, but travelers should take precautions to protect their well-being.

Common health concerns travelers should be aware of

Although Ontario is a relatively safe and health-conscious destination, travelers should be aware of the following potential health issues:

Weather-related health risks:

Dangers in winter:
During periods of extreme cold, frostbite and hypothermia can occur. Travelers should wear appropriate winter clothing, including insulated layers, hats, gloves and waterproof boots.
Slippery sidewalks and streets can pose a fall risk - wear shoes with good traction.

Dangers in summer:

Heat exhaustion and dehydration are common during hot and humid months, especially in urban areas like Toronto. Make sure you stay hydrated, wear light clothing, and seek shade when necessary.

The sun's rays can be particularly intense when visiting lakes or outdoor attractions. Apply sunscreen with at least SPF 30 and wear sunglasses and a hat.

Insect bites and wildlife exposure:
Mosquitoes and ticks can be common in rural and forested areas, especially during spring and summer. To prevent bites, use insect repellent and wear long-sleeved clothing when hiking or camping.
Be aware of Lyme disease, which is transmitted by blacklegged ticks in wooded areas. After outdoor activities, check for ticks and remove them promptly if you find them.

Food and water safety:
Tap water in Ontario is drinkable in all cities and towns. However, when hiking or camping, only drink filtered or bottled water.
Although food standards are high in Ontario, travelers with food allergies should exercise caution when trying new dishes, especially at restaurants that may not accommodate special dietary needs.

Respiratory health:
Air pollution can occur in urban areas, especially in the summer months. Travelers with respiratory illnesses such as asthma should carry their medications and check air quality reports.
Seasonal allergies often occur in spring and fall due to pollen from trees and grasses. Antihistamines can help relieve symptoms.

Emergency services and health options for tourists

Ontario offers an efficient healthcare system with hospitals, clinics and pharmacies readily available in urban and rural areas. However, it is important to understand how to access medical care during your trip.

Emergency numbers:

911 – For emergencies requiring police, fire or rescue services.

Telehealth Ontario: 1-866-797-0000 – A free, 24/7 health consultation service staffed by trained nurses.

Poison Control Center: 1-800-268-9017 – In the event of accidental poisoning or chemical exposure.

Health facilities:

Hospitals: Major cities like Toronto, Ottawa and Hamilton have top-notch hospitals like Toronto General Hospital and Ottawa Hospital. Emergency rooms (ERs) provide emergency care, but wait times can vary.

Outpatient Clinics: For minor injuries or illnesses, outpatient clinics are a convenient option and typically do not require an appointment. They are available in most cities and towns.

Pharmacies: Chains such as Shoppers Drug Mart and Rexall are common and offer over-the-counter medications, prescription refills, and basic medical advice.

Travel Insurance: Tourists should purchase comprehensive travel insurance to cover medical costs as healthcare in Canada can be costly for non-residents.

What to do in a medical emergency:

1. Call 911 if immediate assistance is needed.
2. For non-life-threatening problems, go to the nearest hospital or outpatient clinic.
3. Always carry a copy of your health insurance information with you.

Personal safety tips for different areas in Ontario

Ontario is one of Canada's safest provinces, but as with any travel destination, it's important to remain vigilant and take basic precautions.

Security in major cities (Toronto, Ottawa, Hamilton):

Stay in well-lit and populated places, especially at night.

Be wary of pickpockets in crowded places such as public transport, tourist attractions and events. Keep valuables safe in a shoulder bag or money belt.

Only use licensed taxis or ride-sharing services such as Uber and Lyft.

Avoid isolated areas in city centers after dark and be aware of your surroundings.

Toronto's public transportation (TTC) is safe, but travelers should be vigilant during late hours.

Safety in the countryside and outdoors:

When hiking or exploring Ontario's vast wilderness, always carry a map, compass or GPS device in case of navigation problems.
Let someone know your itinerary before heading to remote areas.
Bring a fully charged phone and portable charger for emergencies.
Look for wildlife like black bears in parks like Algonquin. Store food safely and follow park guidelines.
When hiking in winter, dress appropriately and avoid frozen lakes or rivers unless confirmed safe by local authorities.

Road safety:
Follow Canadian traffic laws, which include driving on the right side of the road.
Be aware of wildlife crossings, especially in northern Ontario.
Winter driving conditions can be dangerous due to snow and ice. If you rent a car in winter, make sure it is equipped with winter tires.
Always wear your seat belt and avoid using your phone while driving.

Safety in public transport:
Public transportation in Ontario is generally safe and reliable. However, remain vigilant and watch out for personal belongings during peak hours.
Use official ticket machines and authorized public transport cards (e.g. PRESTO) to avoid fraud.

If you travel late at night, wait at well-lit and busy train stations.

General travel safety tips:

Keep copies of your important documents (passport, visa, insurance) in a separate location in case of loss.

Avoid sharing your itinerary or hotel details with strangers.

Use hotel safes to store valuables when not in use.

Familiarize yourself with local laws and regulations to avoid accidental violations.

Ontario is a safe and welcoming destination, but travelers should always put their health and safety first. By staying informed, taking precautions and being aware of emergency services, visitors can safely explore Ontario's cities and natural landscapes without unnecessary risks.

Budgeting and payment options

Managing your finances effectively during your trip to Ontario ensures a stress-free experience, whether you're exploring vibrant cities or picturesque rural landscapes. When travelers know how to best exchange money, budget wisely, and choose between payment methods, they can get the most out of their trip.

Best Ways to Exchange and Bank in Ontario

The official currency of Ontario and the rest of Canada is the Canadian dollar (CAD), available in both coins and banknotes. Travelers can exchange or access their money in several ways:

Currency Exchange Options:

The bank:
Major Canadian banks such as RBC (Royal Bank of Canada), TD Canada Trust and Scotiabank offer competitive exchange rates and reliable service.
Banks typically offer cheaper rates than airport kiosks or hotels.
Most cities have branches with 24-hour ATMs.

Cash change machines:
Available at airports, shopping centers and tourist areas, but often with higher fees and less favorable fares.
Only recommended for small last minute replacements.

ATMs (Automated Teller Machines):
Widely used and provide a convenient way to withdraw cash in CAD using international debit or credit cards.
Find out about the fees at both your bank and the ATM provider.
Look for major bank ATMs to avoid third-party surcharges.

Online currency exchange services:
Platforms like Wise (formerly TransferWise) and Revolut offer low-cost exchange rates with minimal fees,

allowing travelers to exchange money digitally before arriving in Ontario.
Tip: Always check exchange rates before exchanging money to avoid unfavorable exchange rates and use ATMs at major banks to minimize transaction fees.

Budget tips for travelers with different spending abilities
Ontario caters to travelers with a range of budgets, from luxury seekers to budget backpackers. How to plan your finances according to different spending levels:

Budget travelers:
Accommodation: Opt for hostels, cheap hotels or vacation rentals through platforms like Airbnb. Look for budget options in neighborhoods outside of downtown.
Eat: Explore food trucks, local markets, and casual restaurants. Supermarkets like No Frills and FreshCo offer affordable, self-sufficient grocery options.
Transportation: Use public transportation like the TTC (Toronto Transit Commission) or regional GO Transit for affordable travel across the province.
Attractions: Many museums and attractions offer free entry days or discounted tickets. Ontario's parks and trails offer excellent free outdoor experiences.
Estimated daily budget: CAD 50-100 per person.

Middle class travelers:
Accommodation: Choose mid-range hotels or boutique accommodations with additional amenities like free

breakfast. Consider well-rated chain hotels such as Holiday Inn or Best Western.
Dining: Enjoy a mix of casual dining and fine dining experiences. Look for local restaurants that offer authentic Canadian cuisine.
Transportation: Consider renting a car for road trips while relying on public transportation in cities.
Attractions: Invest in city passes like the Toronto CityPASS to save on entrance fees to key attractions.
Estimated daily budget: CAD 150-300 per person.

Luxury travelers:
Accommodation: Stay in high-end hotels like The Ritz-Carlton, Fairmont Royal York or luxury resorts in destinations like Muskoka.
Dining: Dine at Michelin-starred restaurants or enjoy curated tasting menus featuring local gourmet cuisine.
Transportation: Hire private chauffeurs, take scenic flights, or book premium rail services for an upscale experience.
Attractions: Opt for private tours and exclusive experiences, such as: B. Winery tours in Niagara-on-the-Lake or spa retreats in Blue Mountain.
Estimated daily budget: CAD 400+ per person.
Tip: Regardless of budget, travelers can save money by planning ahead, booking in advance, and taking advantage of seasonal discounts.

Credit Card vs. Cash: Which Works Best?
Both credit cards and cash have their advantages and disadvantages when traveling in Ontario. When travelers

know where and when to use them, they can manage their expenses more efficiently.

Credit cards:

Widely Accepted: Most establishments, including hotels, restaurants, and stores, accept major credit cards such as Visa, Mastercard, and American Express.

Contactless payments: Tap-to-pay is widely used and makes transactions quick and convenient. Apple Pay and Google Pay are also widely accepted.

Foreign transaction fees: Some cards may charge fees (typically 2-3%) for international transactions - travelers should check with their bank before departure.

Best for: Large purchases, online bookings and emergency expenses.

Tip: For better savings, choose a travel-friendly credit card with no foreign transaction fees.

Box:

Necessary for: Small vendors, markets, tips and some rural areas where card payments may not be accepted.

ATM withdrawals: Convenient for obtaining small amounts of cash when needed, but fees may apply for frequent withdrawals.

Suitable for: Small purchases, tips and emergencies.

Tip: Carry a small amount of cash (50-100 CAD) for everyday expenses, while relying on cards for larger transactions.

Debit cards and prepaid travel cards:

Debit cards: Can be used at ATMs and for direct purchases, but foreign transaction fees may apply.
Prepaid Travel Cards: Allow travelers to pre-load CAD and avoid exchange rate fluctuations while staying within your budget.
Tip: A combination of credit cards, debit cards and some cash offers flexibility and security.

Managing money effectively is crucial to a smooth and enjoyable trip in Ontario. Whether it's currency exchange, budgeting or choosing between payment options, understanding the financial landscape helps travelers avoid unnecessary costs and focus on making the most of their adventure. Travelers should always plan ahead, have emergency funds on hand, and use financial tools like budgeting apps to stay on top of things.

Chapter 5:

Where to stay

Luxury hotels and resorts in Ontario's cities and countryside

Ontario offers a wealth of luxurious accommodations for discerning travelers seeking first-class service, comfort and exclusive experiences. Whether you're looking for a five-star city retreat, a tranquil lakeside resort or a historic hotel with timeless charm, Ontario offers a range of options to enrich any travel experience.

Top luxury accommodations in Ontario

Das Ritz-Carlton, Toronto
Location: Downtown Toronto
Why stay here: This five-star hotel represents elegance and offers breathtaking views of the Toronto skyline and Lake Ontario.

Equipment:
Spacious spa with individual treatments.
Fine dining in the TOCA restaurant with its own cheese cave.
Exclusive club lounge with complimentary gourmet food and drinks.
Spacious rooms with floor-to-ceiling windows and marble bathrooms.

Nearby Attractions: CN Tower, Royal Ontario Museum, Harbourfront.

Fairmont Royal York, Toronto
Location: Toronto, across from Union Station
Why stay here: A historic landmark built in 1929 that combines old-world charm with modern luxury.

Equipment:
Elegant rooms with vintage-inspired decor and modern comforts.
Afternoon tea and good food in the REIGN restaurant.
Indoor pool, fitness center and luxurious spa services.
Direct access to the underground city PATH.
Nearby Attractions: Toronto Eaton Centre, St. Lawrence Market, Scotiabank Arena.

St. Regis Toronto
Location: Downtown Toronto
Why stay here: Known for its impeccable service and personal butler experience.

Equipment:
Unique St. Regis 24-hour butler service.
Luxurious spa with heated saltwater infinity pool.
Opulent rooms with individual furnishings and the latest technology.
Nearby Attractions: Financial District, Distillery District, Art Gallery of Ontario.

Langdon Hall Country House Hotel & Spa

Location: Cambridge, Ontario
Why stay here: A secluded country retreat on a magnificent estate, perfect for relaxation.

Equipment:
Michelin star-worthy restaurant with farm-to-table cuisine.
Full-service spa offering holistic wellness treatments.
Scenic hiking trails, gardens and tranquil forests.
Nearby Attractions: Cambridge Butterfly Conservatory, Grand River.

Das Hazelton Hotel, Toronto
Location: Yorkville, Toronto
Why stay here: A cozy luxury boutique hotel known for celebrity stays and five-star service.

Equipment:
Oversized suites with private balconies and deep soaking tubs.
Spa with exclusive treatments and personalized wellness programs.
Prime location in Yorkville's high-end shopping district.
Nearby Attractions: Royal Ontario Museum, Mink Mile, upscale boutiques.

JW Marriott Thc Rosseau Muskoka Resort & Spa
Location: Muskoka Lakes, Ontario
Why Stay Here: A luxurious lakeside retreat offering outdoor adventure and relaxation.

Equipment:
Waterfront spa with unique treatments inspired by nature.
Private beach access and year-round outdoor activities.
Spacious suites with fireplaces and private balconies.
Nearby Attractions: Muskoka Steamboats, Lake Rosseau, Hiking Trails.

Four Seasons Hotel, Toronto
Location: Yorkville, Toronto
Why stay here: A globally recognized luxury brand that offers impeccable service and first-class amenities.

Equipment:
Michelin-starred restaurant Café Boulud.
Award-winning spa and wellness center.
Rooms with panoramic city views and modern elegance.
Nearby Attractions: High-end shopping, cultural attractions on Bloor Street.

What amenities can travelers expect in high-end accommodations?
Luxury hotels and resorts in Ontario go beyond basic comforts to offer personalized service and exceptional experiences. Here's what travelers can expect when booking a high-end stay:

World-class culinary experiences
On-site gourmet restaurants with internationally recognized chefs.

Menus made from regional ingredients with wine pairings and tasting menus.
Private dining options and exclusive culinary experiences.

State-of-the-art wellness and spa facilities
Unique spa treatments including massages, facials and holistic therapies.
Heated indoor and outdoor pools, hot tubs and saunas.
Fully equipped fitness center with personal trainers and yoga sessions.

Personal concierge service
Dedicated concierge teams are available to assist with reservations, transportation and experiences.
Tailored itineraries and recommendations tailored to guests' preferences.
Exclusive access to events, tours and VIP experiences.

Generous room facilities
Spacious suites with luxurious linens, high-quality linens and fine furnishings.
Smart room technology, including touch-controlled lighting and climate settings.
Designer toiletries, deep soaking tubs, and rainfall showers.

Exclusive activities and excursions
Private yacht charters, helicopter tours and luxury car rentals.

Guided cultural tours, wine tastings and outdoor adventures.
Seasonal activities such as golfing, skiing and wildlife safaris.

Seamless business and event facilities
High-tech meeting rooms and event spaces for corporate and social gatherings.
Executive lounges with complimentary refreshments and workstations.
High-speed WiFi and business concierge services.

Tips for booking luxury stays in Ontario
Book early: Popular hotels fill up quickly, especially during peak seasons and events.

Look for package deals: Many luxury hotels offer seasonal packages that include spa treatments, dining vouchers, or activity discounts.
Join loyalty programs: Sign up for hotel loyalty programs and enjoy perks like room upgrades, late check-outs, and exclusive offers.
Consider traveling off-peak: Luxury stays can be cheaper in the off-peak seasons (spring and fall).

Ontario's luxury hotels and resorts provide a relaxing retreat for travelers seeking comfort, exceptional service and unforgettable experiences. Whether you enjoy the cosmopolitan charm of Toronto or the tranquil beauty of the Muskoka Lakes, world-class accommodations will meet your every need and make your stay in Ontario an unforgettable experience.

Mid-range accommodations: comfort meets affordability

Ontario offers a variety of mid-range accommodation that strikes a balance of comfort, convenience and affordability. Whether you're traveling to bustling cities like Toronto and Ottawa or exploring scenic rural areas like Muskoka or Prince Edward County, mid-range hotels offer great value with modern amenities and family-friendly features.

Affordable yet comfortable hotel options in major cities and rural areas

Travelers looking for a budget-conscious yet stylish stay will find plenty of options across Ontario. Here are some recommended mid-range hotels that offer excellent service, comfortable rooms and convenient locations at a reasonable price.

Best Western Premier Toronto Airport Carlingview Hotel

Location: Toronto (near Pearson International Airport)

Why stay here: A great option for travelers looking for easy access to the airport and connectivity to the city.

Equipment:

Free airport shuttle service and parking.

Indoor pool and fitness center.
On-site restaurant with diverse menu options.
Nearby Attractions: Toronto Congress Centre, Centennial Park Conservatory.

Holiday Inn Toronto Downtown Centre
Location: Toronto
Why stay here: Located near the lively Yonge Dundas Square, ideal for sightseeing.

Equipment:
Modern rooms with work areas and free WiFi.
Indoor pool and fitness center.
On-site dining and proximity to public transport.
Nearby Attractions: Eaton Centre, Royal Ontario Museum, St. Lawrence Market.

Courtyard by Marriott Ottawa Downtown
Location: Ottawa
Why stay here: Offers comfort and convenience in the heart of Canada's capital.

Equipment:

Spacious rooms with ergonomic workstations.
Indoor pool and 24-hour fitness center.
Popular attractions and restaurants are within walking distance.
Nearby Attractions: Parliament Hill, Rideau Canal, ByWard Market.

Residence Inn by Marriott Niagara Falls

Location: Niagara Falls
Why stay here: Perfect for families and extended stays, with suite-style accommodations.

Equipment:
Fully equipped kitchens in every suite.
Free breakfast buffet.
Indoor pool and children's playground.
Nearby Attractions: Niagara Falls, Clifton Hill, Fallsview Casino.

Sandman Hotel Hamilton
Location: Hamilton
Why stay here: A reliable mid-range option for business and leisure travelers.

Equipment:
Modern rooms with kitchenettes and comfortable beds.
On-site dining and fitness facilities.
Close to major highways and public transportation.
Nearby Attractions: Royal Botanical Gardens, African Lion Safari.

Super 8 by Wyndham Peterborough
Standort: Peterborough
Why stay here: Affordable and comfortable accommodation ideal for travelers exploring the Kawarthas.

Equipment:
Free breakfast and WiFi.
Heated indoor pool and hot tub.
Pet friendly rooms available.
Nearby Attractions: Trent-Severn Waterway, Riverview Park and Zoo.

Hilton Garden Inn Sudbury

Location: Sudbury
Why stay here: A great mid-range option in northern Ontario with modern amenities and easy access to natural attractions.

Equipment:
Fitness center and indoor pool.
On-site restaurant serving locally inspired dishes.
Spacious rooms with ergonomic work areas.
Nearby Attractions: Science North, Dynamic Earth, Lake Laurentian Conservation Area.

Recommendations for family-friendly stays
Traveling with family requires accommodations that offer extra space, kid-friendly amenities and a welcoming atmosphere. Here are some great mid-range hotels that are perfect for family stays:

Staybridge Suites Toronto - Vaughan South
Why Families Love It: Offers spacious suites with full kitchens, perfect for extended stays.

Kid-Friendly Amenities: Free Breakfast, Family Suites, Outdoor BBQ Area.
Nearby attractions: Canada's Wonderland, LEGOLAND Discovery Centre.

TownePlace Suites by Marriott London
Why families love it: Pet-friendly and large rooms with kitchenettes.
Kid-Friendly Amenities: Free continental breakfast, board games available.
Nearby Attractions: Storybook Gardens, Fanshawe Pioneer Village.

Homewood Suites by Hilton Cambridge-Waterloo
Why Families Love It: Offers homey comfort with spacious two-bedroom suites.
Kid-friendly amenities: indoor pool, free evening snacks, outdoor patio with grill.
Nearby Attractions: African Lion Safari, Cambridge Butterfly Conservatory.

Delta Hotels by Marriott Kingston Waterfront
Why families love it: Stunning waterfront location with harbor view rooms.
Kid-Friendly Amenities: Heated indoor pool, free WiFi, and family packages.
Nearby Attractions: Fort Henry, Kingston 1000 Islands Cruises.

Fairfield Inn & Suites by Marriott Thunder Bay

Why families love it: Quiet suburban location with plenty of outdoor space nearby.
Kid-Friendly Amenities: Free hot breakfast, indoor pool.
Nearby Attractions: Terry Fox Monument, Sleeping Giant Provincial Park.

What to expect from mid-range accommodation in Ontario

Travelers who choose mid-range hotels can expect a mix of affordability and comfort, as well as amenities to make their stay enjoyable. Here's what awaits you:
Comfortable rooms: Spacious rooms with modern furnishings, free Wi-Fi and flat-screen TVs.
On-site dining: Many hotels have on-site restaurants or free breakfast options.
Fitness and leisure facilities: gyms, pools and sometimes spa services.
Business Facilities: Meeting rooms, work areas and conference facilities for business travelers.
Great Locations: Close to major attractions and transportation hubs.
Friendly Service: Reliable and helpful staff offering travel tips and assistance.

Tips for booking mid-range accommodation

Book early in peak season: prices can rise quickly during popular travel periods.
Look for family packages: Some hotels offer special deals for children, including free meals or discounted rates.

Read guest reviews: Sites like TripAdvisor and Google Reviews can provide insight into cleanliness and service quality.
Look for free perks: Free breakfast, Wi-Fi, and parking can save you money.
Consider options for longer stays: If you're traveling for more than a few days, suite hotels with kitchenettes can be cost-effective.

Ontario's mid-range accommodations offer travelers the perfect combination of affordability and convenience without sacrificing comfort. Whether you're traveling with family, for business or on a cross-provincial road trip, there's a suitable option that offers great value and easy access to Ontario's top attractions.

Budget-friendly stays: hostels, B&Bs and unique accommodations

Ontario offers a variety of affordable accommodations that allow travelers to explore the province without breaking the bank. From hostels in vibrant city centers to charming guesthouses in picturesque rural areas, there are plenty of affordable options. Travelers can also find unique accommodation experiences like cozy cabins and Airbnb rentals that offer comfort and value.

The best hostels and guesthouses in all of Ontario

For budget-conscious travelers, hostels and guesthouses offer a great way to save money while enjoying a sociable atmosphere and convenient location. Here are some top-rated options across the province:

Toronto:

Planet Traveller Hostel
Why stay here: Eco-friendly, vibrant atmosphere with modern amenities.

Key Features:
Free breakfast and rooftop terrace with city views.
Dormitory and private room options.
Close to Kensington Market and Queen Street West.

The only Backpackers Inn
Why stay here: Quirky and cozy, with a cafe and bar on site.

Key Features:
Free breakfast included.
Located close to the subway connection for easy travel.
Social events and communal kitchen.

Ottawa:
HI Ottawa Jail Hostel
Why stay here: A unique experience in a former prison-turned-hostel.

Key Features:

Historical ambience with themed rooms.
Parliament Hill and ByWard Market are within walking distance.
Free breakfast and tours.
Auberge des Arts Bed and Breakfast
Why stay here: Affordable and charming stay close to major attractions.

Key Features:
Cozy, family atmosphere.
Free WiFi and breakfast included.
Close to museums and historical attractions.

Niagara Falls:
Hostelling International Niagara Falls
Why stay here: Ideal for travelers looking for budget accommodation near the falls.

Key Features:
Free coffee and tea.
Social events and group outings.
Proximity to Niagara Parkway and Clifton Hill attractions.
Niagara Inn Bed & Breakfast
Why stay here: A comfortable and affordable B&B option.

Key Features:
Homemade breakfast.
Quiet environment, perfect for relaxing.
Easy access to the waterfalls and wineries.

Muskoka:
Muskoka Lakes Hostel
Why stay here: Budget-friendly accommodation in the middle of nature.

Key Features:
Rustic charm with scenic lake views.
Hiking and canoeing opportunities nearby.
Affordable dorm and private room options.

Kingston:
Hochelaga Inn
Why stay here: Historic guesthouse with affordable rates.

Key Features:
Charming Victorian-style rooms.
The waterfront and downtown are within walking distance.
Free breakfast and free parking.

Tips for finding accommodation deals

Traveling on a budget doesn't mean sacrificing comfort or convenience. Here are some tips to help you find the best accommodation deals:

Book in advance: Secure cheaper rates by booking several weeks or months in advance, especially during peak tourist seasons.

Use price comparison websites: Platforms like Booking.com, Hostelworld and Expedia often offer discounted prices and user reviews.
Look for loyalty programs: Many hotel chains and booking websites offer reward points and discounts for repeat bookings.
Travel outside of peak season: Prices drop significantly in late fall and early spring, when tourist numbers are lower.
Consider midweek stays: Hotel prices tend to be lower on weekdays than on weekends.
Stay outside city centers: Suburban accommodation is often cheaper and offers good transport links to major attractions.
Use Budget Travel Apps: Apps like Hostelworld, Couchsurfing and Airbnb can help you find affordable and unique stays.
Look for Discounts: Discounts for students, seniors, and groups are often available at many properties.

Unique accommodation experiences: cabins, Airbnb and more

Ontario offers a variety of unique, affordable accommodations that go beyond traditional hotels and hostels. Here are some alternative accommodation options:

Cozy cabins and cottages:

Perfect for nature lovers and those looking for a quiet retreat.

Recommended locations:
Algonquin Provincial Park: Cabins with stunning lake views and access to hiking trails.
Bruce Peninsula: Affordable log cabins near the crystal clear waters of Georgian Bay.
Kawartha Lakes: Budget-friendly cottages for weekend getaways.

Airbnb and vacation rentals:
Airbnb offers travelers the opportunity to stay in unique accommodations, including private homes, apartments and tiny houses, at cheaper prices than hotels.

Tips for Budget Airbnb Stays:
Book entire houses for larger groups to save money.
Opt for stays with kitchens to prepare meals and reduce food costs.
Look for properties with flexible cancellation policies and discounts for longer stays.

University residences (seasonal stays):
Many universities in Ontario, such as the University of Toronto and Queen's University, offer affordable, dorm-style accommodation during the summer months.

Advantages:
Affordable accommodation with access to campus amenities.
Convenient locations close to city centers.
Add meal plan options often.

Farm stays:
Experience Ontario's rural charm with a stay on a working farm.
Advantages:
Fresh, locally sourced meals are included in the stay.
Opportunities to participate in agricultural activities.
Affordable and family friendly options.

What to expect from budget accommodation in Ontario
Travelers staying in budget accommodations can expect:
Basic amenities: Clean rooms, Wi-Fi access, and shared or private bathrooms.
Social atmosphere: Hostels and guesthouses often offer common areas for meeting other travelers.
Self-Catering Options: Many accommodations have kitchens, which can reduce food costs.
Limited luxury amenities: Budget accommodations focus on practicality rather than luxury, but still provide a comfortable experience.

Ontario offers a diverse selection of affordable accommodation, from urban hostels to rural cabins and Airbnb stays. Whether you are traveling alone, with friends or with family, there are many affordable options to ensure a comfortable and enjoyable trip without spending too much. By planning ahead and exploring unique accommodation experiences, travelers can make the most of their Ontario adventure while staying within their budget.

Chapter 6:

Transportation and locomotion

Airports and major entry points

Ontario is well connected to domestic and international destinations through its extensive airport network. Whether traveling from abroad or within Canada, travelers will find convenient entry points with various transportation options to reach their final destination.

Major international and regional airports in Ontario

Ontario has several major airports that serve as important entry points for travelers. Below are the most important ones:

Toronto Pearson International Airport (YYZ)

Location: Mississauga, approximately 22 km from downtown Toronto.

Key Features:

Canada's busiest airport with direct flights to over 180 destinations worldwide.

Offers two terminals (T1 and T3) with extensive dining, shopping and business facilities.

Important hub for Air Canada and WestJet.

Transportation options from Pearson Airport:

UP Express Train: Direct connection to Union Station in downtown Toronto in 25 minutes.
TTC Public Transportation: Buses 900 Airport Express and 52A serve various areas of the city.
Taxis/Rideshares: Uber, Lyft and airport taxis are available to downtown at fixed rates.
Car rental: Multiple providers including Avis, Hertz and Enterprise.

Billy Bishop Toronto City Airport (YTZ)
Location: Downtown Toronto, on the Toronto Islands.
Key Features:
Ideal for short-haul domestic flights and select US routes.
Operated primarily by Porter Airlines, it offers a boutique flying experience.
Its close proximity to downtown Toronto makes it a popular destination for business travelers.

Transportation options from Billy Bishop Airport:
Airport Shuttle: Free shuttle to Union Station (15-minute ride).
Ferry Service: A short ferry ride connects the airport to the mainland.
Taxis/Rideshares: Available at the terminal entrance.
On foot: The pedestrian tunnel provides direct access to downtown Toronto.

Ottawa Macdonald-Cartier International Airport (YOW)

Location: 10 km south of downtown Ottawa.

Key Features:
The main airport serving Canada's capital city with international and domestic connections.
Well equipped for business and leisure travelers.
Hub for government and diplomatic travel.

Transportation options from Ottawa Airport:
OC Transpo Bus: Route 97 provides service to downtown Ottawa.
Taxis/Ride-Sharing: Taxis and ride-sharing services are available at a fixed price.
Car rental: Several car rental companies in the terminal.

Hamilton International Airport (YHM)
Location: Hamilton, approximately 60 km from Toronto.
Key Features:
A growing alternative for budget travelers with low-cost airlines such as Swoop Airlines.
Convenient for access to the Niagara Region and southwestern Ontario.

Transportation options from Hamilton Airport:
GO Transit: Bus connection to Toronto and surrounding areas.
Car rental and taxis: Available at the airport terminal.
Ride Sharing: Uber and Lyft services operate in the area.

Thunder Bay International Airport (YQT)

Location: Northwestern Ontario, 5 km from Thunder Bay city center.

Key Features:
Serves as a gateway to outdoor adventure destinations like Lake Superior.
Offers flights to major Canadian hubs including Toronto and Winnipeg.

Transportation options from Thunder Bay Airport:
City Transit: Local bus service to downtown and surrounding neighborhoods.
Car rental and taxis: Available in the terminal.
Shuttle service: Offered by some hotels and tour operators.

Other regional airports
Ontario also has several smaller airports for regional and domestic travel, including:
London International Airport (YXU): Serves southwestern Ontario with connections to Toronto, Calgary and leisure destinations.
Windsor International Airport (YQG): Convenient for travelers to and from Detroit, Michigan.
Sudbury Airport (YSB): Major access point for the mining industry and outdoor tourism in northern Ontario.

Transport options from airports to city centers

When arriving at Ontario airports, travelers have several options to reach their destination conveniently and cost-effectively.

Public transportation:
Toronto Pearson: The UP Express train provides direct service to Union Station.
Ottawa Airport: OC Transpo bus routes connect the airport to important locations in the city.
Thunder Bay Airport: City transport services provide affordable transportation options.

Taxis and rideshare services:
Available at all major airports with regulated fare systems.
Toronto Pearson offers flat rate taxi services to major city areas.
Rideshare services such as Uber and Lyft are available at most airports.

Airport shuttle service:
Many hotels offer free or paid shuttle services to and from airports.
Shuttle services to Niagara Falls operate from Toronto airports.

Car rental:
There are rental agencies at all major airports, offering convenient access to road trips and self-drive explorations.

Booking in advance can help you secure better rates, especially during peak travel times.

Tips for travelers arriving in Ontario

Plan your transport in advance: Research the best transportation option to your destination to save time and avoid last-minute costs.
Use prepaid public transport cards: Many cities, including Toronto, offer transit cards like the PRESTO card for buses, trains and subways.
Pay attention to peak times: Airports can be crowded during morning and evening rush hours; Plan accordingly for a smoother trip.
Consider airport hotels: If you have a longer layover, airport hotels offer comfortable stays with shuttle service to the terminals.
Stay informed: Use airport websites and mobile apps to stay up to date on flight status, transportation schedules and terminal maps.

Ontario's airports offer travelers excellent connectivity and efficient transportation options. Whether you're arriving in bustling Toronto or exploring the natural beauty of Northern Ontario, planning your transportation in advance will ensure your trip gets off to a smooth start.

Public transport: buses, trains and subways

Ontario has a well-developed public transportation system that makes it easier for travelers to get around cities and regions efficiently. Whether you're exploring busy metropolitan areas like Toronto or traveling between cities, public transportation is affordable, reliable and accessible.

How to navigate Ontario's public transit system

Ontario's public transportation system consists of buses, trains, trams and subways. The main transit providers include:

Toronto Transit Commission (TTC)

Coverage area: Toronto and surrounding suburbs.

Means of transport:

Subway: Four main lines covering major areas such as downtown, midtown and suburban areas.

Trams: Iconic red trams on busy routes, especially in downtown Toronto.

Buses: Extensive network covering areas not served by subway or tram lines.

Important subway lines:

Line 1 (Yonge-University): Connects downtown Toronto with North York.

Line 2 (Bloor-Danforth): East-west coverage from Etobicoke to Scarborough.

Line 3 (Scarborough RT): Connecting eastern districts.

Line 4 (Sheppard): Serves areas of northern Toronto.

Tips for using TTC:

Purchase a PRESTO card for easy tap-on, tap-off travel across the TTC network.
Use the Rocket Man or Transit app to track real-time schedules.
Avoid peak hours (7am-9am and 4pm-7pm) to ensure a more comfortable journey.

GO Transit
Coverage area: Greater Toronto Area (GTA) and beyond, connecting cities such as Hamilton, Niagara Falls, Kitchener and Barrie.
Means of transport:
GO Trains: Long-distance trains with comfortable seating and bike-friendly coaches.
GO buses: Connect cities and suburbs not served by rail routes.
Popular GO Transit Routes:
Toronto to Niagara Falls for a scenic getaway.
Toronto to Hamilton, an affordable and convenient alternative to the car.
Weekend excursion trains to attractions like Blue Mountain and Algonquin Park.
Tips for using GO Transit:
Purchase tickets via the GO Transit app or at station kiosks.
Weekend and group tickets offer discounts for multiple riders.
Check schedules carefully as service may be less frequent on weekends.

OC Transpo (Ottawa)

Coverage area: Ottawa and surrounding areas, with service to Gatineau, Quebec.

Means of transport:
O-Train Light Rail Transit (LRT): The city's rapid transit system with the Trillium and Confederation lines.
Buses: Extensive network that reaches all parts of the city and government districts.

Tips for using OC Transpo:
Purchase a Presto card or use the OC Transpo app for easy travel.
Park-and-ride facilities make it convenient for those staying outside the city.
The LRT offers a quick way to reach major attractions such as Parliament Hill and ByWard Market.

Other regional transport systems
Several cities in Ontario have their own public transportation networks that are travel-friendly:
Mississauga (MiWay): Bus service with connections to GO Transit and TTC.
Brampton Transit: Known for the Züm express bus service to Toronto.
Waterloo Region (GRT): Includes light rail (ION) and buses, ideal for exploring Kitchener-Waterloo.
Hamilton Street Railway (HSR): Extensive bus routes connecting to GO Transit services.
London Transit (LTC): Covers the city with regular and express services.

Tip: Most regional transportation systems accept the PRESTO card for seamless transfers.

Passports and apps make commuting easier

PRESTO-Karte

A reloadable smart card used for fare payments on multiple transit systems, including TTC, GO Transit and OC Transpo.

Available at subway stations, online and at Shoppers Drug Mart locations.

Offers daily and monthly pass options for frequent travelers.

Advantages:

Practical tap-on/tap-off system.

Automatically calculates the best rate for transfers.

Discounts for seniors and students.

Public transport and navigation apps

Using mobile apps can make getting around Ontario easier and more efficient.

Transit app: Provides real-time bus and train tracking for multiple cities in Ontario.

Rocket Man: Ideal for TTC users, with live updates on bus and subway arrivals.

OC Transpo App: Ottawa's official transit app with trip planning and real-time information.

GO Transit app: schedules, fare information and ticket purchasing for GO services.

Google Maps: Comprehensive trip planning with accurate transit routes and times.
Tip: Download your favorite app before your trip and enable service alert notifications.

Tips for using public transportation in Ontario

Plan your routes in advance: Use trip planners available on public transportation websites or apps to avoid delays and confusion.
Avoid rush hours: Public transportation can be crowded during rush hours. Therefore, travel during off-peak hours.
Accessibility Considerations: Most transportation systems have accessible vehicles and stations for travelers with mobility needs.
Keep change for buses: In some regions, buses do not offer change if you pay with cash.
Know Transfer Policies: Some transportation systems allow free transfers within a certain time period; If necessary, ask for a transfer receipt.
Stay up to date on service changes: Weather conditions or construction may impact schedules - stay up to date via apps or websites.

Ontario's public transportation system provides an efficient and affordable way to get around the province. Whether traveling within cities like Toronto or traveling between regions using GO Transit, travelers can move easily across Ontario with the right passes and apps. By planning ahead and taking advantage of available transportation options, visitors can enjoy a stress-free experience.

Car rentals, ride-sharing and alternative travel options

Exploring Ontario offers a range of transportation options, from renting a car for road trips to using convenient rideshare services and intercity buses. Depending on your travel plans—whether you stay in urban centers or venture into the vast countryside—choosing the right mode of transportation can greatly enrich your trip.

Is it worth renting a car to explore Ontario?
Renting a car in Ontario can be a good choice for travelers who want to explore major cities and visit attractions in remote areas. Ontario's expansive geography, scenic road trip routes, and well-developed highways make driving a convenient option. However, for city travelers, public transportation and ride-sharing may be more convenient.

Benefits of renting a car:
Freedom to Explore: Perfect for visiting national parks, rural towns and remote destinations like Algonquin Park or Prince Edward County.
Scenic Road Trips: Famous routes like the Niagara Parkway, the Bruce Peninsula and the Trans-Canada Highway offer breathtaking views.

Convenience for Groups: If you are traveling with family or friends, renting a car can be cost-effective.
Flexibility: Avoid rigid bus or train timetables and make spontaneous stops along the way.

Possible disadvantages:
Traffic in cities: Toronto and Ottawa experience heavy traffic congestion and parking can be expensive and limited.
Cost: Gas prices, insurance, and parking fees can add up, especially in urban areas.
Winter Driving Challenges: Ontario winters can bring snow and ice, which can be challenging for unfamiliar drivers.

Top car rental companies in Ontario:
Enterprise Rent-A-Car (multiple locations in cities and airports)
Hertz (offers road trip packages and one-way rentals)
Budget Car Rental (affordable options for travelers)
Avis (convenient airport and city center locations)

Tips for Renting a Car in Ontario:
Book in advance: Prices can fluctuate, especially during peak tourist seasons.
Look for discounts: Take advantage of memberships like AAA or CAA for rental discounts.
Consider insurance: Some credit cards offer rental protection – check before purchasing additional insurance.

Know the traffic rules: In Ontario, traffic drives on the right and wearing seat belts is mandatory.
Toll Schedule: Some highways, such as Highway 407 (ETR), are toll roads and use electronic billing.

Ridesharing (Uber, Lyft)

For short trips within cities, rideshare services like Uber and Lyft offer a hassle-free way to get around without the need for a rental car.

Advantages of ride sharing:

Cost-effective for short distances: Ideal for quick trips through the city.
Convenience: Easily book rides via mobile apps without having to worry about parking.
Availability: Widely available in major cities such as Toronto, Ottawa and Hamilton.
Diverse options: Choose between affordable rides and luxurious services.

Disadvantages of ride sharing:

Price increases: Prices may increase during peak periods and special events.
Limited in remote areas: Availability may be scarce in rural or smaller towns.

Tips for using ride sharing services:

Download the app and set it up in advance to avoid connection issues.
Before booking, compare prices between Uber and Lyft.

Use the fare sharing feature when traveling with friends to split the cost.

Intercity buses (Greyhound, Megabus, Ontario Northland)

Intercity buses are an affordable and comfortable way to travel between Ontario's cities and regions, especially for those who would rather not drive. These services are well connected and offer reliable schedules and amenities such as WiFi and onboard toilets.

Major bus routes in Ontario:

Megabus

Budget-friendly long-distance travel between major cities like Toronto, Ottawa and Kingston.

Amenities include free WiFi, power sockets and toilets on board.

Tickets can be purchased online with a pre-sale discount.

Ontario Northland

Offers connections to northern Ontario destinations such as Sudbury, North Bay and Timmins.

Comfortable sofas with reclining seats and plenty of luggage space.

Ideal for travelers exploring the wilderness or remote towns.

FlixBus

Recently launched services connect Toronto with nearby cities at competitive rates.

Environmentally friendly buses with flexible booking options.

Trainer Canada

Offers cross-border routes to U.S. destinations such as New York and Buffalo.

Comfortable seating and reliable departure schedules.

GO Transitbusse

Provides regional connections within the Greater Toronto and Hamilton Area (GTHA).

Ideal for travelers moving between suburbs and city centers.

Tips for using intercity buses:

Book tickets in advance to get the best rates.

Arrive at the bus station early to ensure a smooth boarding.

Pack light as baggage allowance may be limited.

Alternative transportation options

For travelers who prefer other ways to get around Ontario, several alternative options may be considered:

Carpool services:

Websites and apps like Poparide allow travelers to share rides with locals traveling in the same direction, reducing costs and environmental impact.

Ride a bike:

Cities like Toronto and Ottawa have extensive bike networks with bike-sharing services like Bike Share Toronto and VeloGO.

Ideal for eco-friendly travelers exploring the city center.

Train travel:
VIA Rail offers scenic train rides across Ontario, connecting Toronto to cities like Windsor, London and Kingston.
Comfortable for long-distance travel with scenic views along the way.
Ferries:
Ferries run to destinations like the Toronto Islands, Pelee Island, and Manitoulin Island, offering a scenic alternative to driving.

Ontario offers a variety of transportation options to suit different travel styles and needs. For road trips and exploring remote areas, a rental car is ideal, while ridesharing and public transportation are convenient for traveling around the city. Budget-conscious travelers can use intercity buses, and eco-friendly options like cycling and carpooling offer sustainable alternatives. Whatever you decide, planning ahead and choosing the right mode of transportation will ensure a smooth and enjoyable journey through Ontario.

Chapter 7:

Must-see tourist attractions

Iconic Landmarks: Niagara Falls, CN Tower and more

Ontario is home to some of Canada's most famous and impressive landmarks, attracting millions of visitors each year. From natural wonders to architectural marvels, these must-see attractions offer a glimpse into Ontario's rich history, culture and breathtaking landscapes.

Niagara Falls: A Natural Wonder

Why it's a must:
Niagara Falls, one of the most famous waterfalls in the world, lies on the border between Ontario and New York. The sheer power and beauty of the cascading waters make it a bucket list destination for travelers from around the world.

Top experiences at Niagara Falls:
Hornblower Cruise: Get up close to the roaring waterfalls on a boat ride.
Journey Behind the Falls: Explore tunnels that lead to viewing platforms just behind the falls.

Skylon Tower: Enjoy panoramic views from an observation deck above the falls.
Niagara Parkway: Scenic drive with scenic stops along the Niagara River.

Tips for avoiding crowds:
Visit us early morning or late afternoon to avoid the crowds.
Plan a trip in the off-season (spring or fall) to expect fewer tourists and pleasant weather.
Consider an overnight stay to enjoy the waterfalls illuminated at night without the daytime crowds.

Attractions nearby:
Niagara-on-the-Lake: A charming city known for wineries and historic sites.
Clifton Hill: Entertainment district with attractions like the Niagara SkyWheel and fun museums.

CN Tower: A sky-high experience

Why it's a must:
At 553 meters (1,815 feet) tall, the CN Tower dominates Toronto's skyline and offers unparalleled views of the city and beyond. Once the tallest free-standing structure in the world, it is a must-see for its engineering marvels and exhilarating experiences.

Top experiences at CN Tower:
EdgeWalk: An exciting, hands-free walk around the outer edge of the tower.

Glass Floor: Walk on the transparent floor and look directly at the streets below.
360 Restaurant: Dine at a rotating restaurant with breathtaking views of Toronto and Lake Ontario.
Observation Deck: Enjoy breathtaking views of the Toronto skyline, especially at sunset.

Tips for avoiding crowds:
Book tickets online in advance to avoid long lines.
Visit us on weekdays and during off-peak hours (early morning or late evening).
Combine with nearby attractions like Ripley's Aquarium or Rogers Center to maximize your visit.

Attractions nearby:
Harbourfront Centre: A lively waterfront promenade with cultural events, parks and restaurants.
Distillery District: A historic district with cobblestone streets, artisan shops and art galleries.

Parliament Hill: A Symbol of Canadian Heritage

Why it's a must:
Located in Ottawa, Parliament Hill is the heart of Canadian democracy and a breathtaking architectural masterpiece. The large neo-Gothic buildings house the country's federal government and provide insights into Canada's political history.

Top experiences on Parliament Hill:

Changing of the Guard: Experience this ceremonial event during the summer months.
Tours: Explore Center Block and learn about Canadian governance and history.
Sound and Light Show: A dazzling multimedia show projected onto the Parliament buildings in summer.
Winter Lights Across Canada: A seasonal light show that brightens the hill during the holidays.

Tips for avoiding crowds:
Arrive early to secure a good spot for the changing of the guard.
Visit us in the morning for quieter tours.
Use virtual tours when physical access is limited during renovations.

Attractions nearby:
Rideau Canal: A UNESCO World Heritage Site, ideal for boating or skating in winter.
ByWard Market: A lively area full of local shops, restaurants and galleries.

More iconic landmarks to explore

Casa Loma (Toronto): A majestic Gothic Revival-style castle that offers a glimpse into Toronto's rich past, complete with secret tunnels, beautiful gardens and panoramic city views.
Royal Ontario Museum (Toronto): One of the largest museums in North America with extensive exhibitions of art, culture and natural history.

Thousand Islands (Eastern Ontario): A stunning archipelago in the St. Lawrence River known for scenic boat trips and historic castles like Boldt Castle.
Algonquin Provincial Park (Zentral-Ontario): An outdoor enthusiast's paradise with pristine lakes, hiking trails and abundant wildlife including moose and bears.
Stratford Festival (Stratford): A world-renowned theater festival celebrating Shakespeare and contemporary plays.
Science North (Sudbury): An interactive science museum with exciting exhibitions on mining, space and natural sciences, ideal for families.

Ontario's landmarks offer something for every traveler, from the awe-inspiring power of Niagara Falls to the sky-high thrill of the CN Tower to the rich political heritage of Parliament Hill. Whether you're looking for adventure, history, or cultural immersion, these must-see attractions should be at the top of your itinerary.

Pro Tips for Exploring Famous Landmarks:

Purchase city passes to receive discounts at multiple attractions.
Plan visits during off-peak hours to avoid crowds.
Look for guided tours to gain deeper insight and historical context.

National parks and outdoor excursions

Ontario is home to an incredible variety of natural wonders, from pristine lakes and dense forests to dramatic cliffs and parks teeming with wildlife. Whether you're an outdoor enthusiast or a casual traveler looking to connect with nature, Ontario offers endless opportunities for adventure and relaxation.

Bruce Peninsula: A Scenic Escape

Why it's a must:

The Bruce Peninsula, located between Georgian Bay and Lake Huron, is known for its rugged cliffs, turquoise waters and lush forests. It is a paradise for hikers, campers and photographers alike.

Top attractions and activities:

The Grotto: A stunning sea cave with crystal clear blue waters, perfect for swimming and photography.

Bruce Trail: Canada's longest and oldest footpath, offering breathtaking views along the escarpment.

Fathom Five National Marine Park: Explore shipwrecks and underwater caves with snorkeling or glass-bottom boat tours.

Flowerpot Island: A short boat ride away, known for its unique rock formations and hiking trails.

Travel tips:

Book parking or shuttle passes in advance during peak summer months.

Visit the city in the fall and enjoy fewer crowds and stunning fall colors.

Bring water shoes for rocky shores and uneven terrain.

Muskoka Lakes: Cottage Country Paradise

Why it's a must:

Often referred to as "Cottage Country," Muskoka is a popular summer destination for those seeking waterside relaxation, outdoor recreation and luxurious lakeside living.

Top attractions and activities:

Boat Trips: Take a scenic cruise on Lake Muskoka, Lake Rosseau or Lake Joseph.

Water Sports: Enjoy kayaking, paddling and fishing in the calm waters.

Hiking Trails: Explore hiking trails like Huckleberry Rock Lookout for panoramic views.

Resorts and Spas: Relax at premier lakeside resorts like Deerhurst Resort.

Travel tips:

Summer is the high season; Book your accommodation well in advance.

Fall offers beautiful foliage and fewer crowds.

Many restaurants and attractions are closed during the winter months, so plan accordingly.

Algonquin Provincial Park: A wilderness wonderland

Why it's a must:
Algonquin Park is Ontario's premier outdoor adventure destination with over 7,600 square kilometers of forests, lakes and rivers. It is ideal for hiking, canoeing and wildlife watching.

Top attractions and activities:
Canoeing and Kayaking: Paddle through a vast network of lakes and rivers, offering backcountry camping opportunities.
Hiking Trails: Hiking trails like the Lookout Trail offer panoramic views, while the Barron Canyon Trail showcases towering cliffs.
Wildlife viewing: Discover moose, beavers, wolves and black bears in their natural habitat.
Visitor Centers: Learn about the park's ecology and indigenous heritage.

Travel tips:
In the summer, bring insect repellent for mosquitoes and black flies.
A permit is required for camping and backcountry activities. So book early.
Algonquin's fall colors are world-famous, making September and October ideal for visits.

Thousand Islands: A River Wonderland

Why it's a must:

Located along the St. Lawrence River, the Thousand Islands region features more than 1,800 small islands that offer scenic boat tours and charming waterfront communities.

Top attractions and activities:

Boldt Castle: A romantic, historic castle only accessible by boat.

Boat Trips: Sightseeing tours offer breathtaking views of the islands and their magnificent houses.

Fishing and Kayaking: Excellent ways to explore the calm waters and hidden coves.

Bike Trails: The Thousand Islands Parkway offers scenic bike trails.

Travel tips:

Cross the border to explore both the Canadian and US sides of the river.

Summer offers the best weather, but fall cruises are spectacular.

Look out for local specialties like freshly caught fish and maple snacks.

Niagara Escarpment: A UNESCO Biosphere Reserve

Why it's a must:

Stretching 725 kilometers, the Niagara Escarpment is a breathtaking natural feature with dramatic cliffs, waterfalls and scenic vistas. It is a perfect place for hiking and photography.

Top attractions and activities:
Webster's Falls and Tews Falls: Beautiful waterfalls in the Hamilton area, known as the "Waterfall Capital of the World."
Rattlesnake Point: A popular hiking and climbing destination with breathtaking views.
Caving: Visit the Scenic Caves near Collingwood for underground adventures.
Apple Pie Trail: A foodie journey through orchards and ciderries in the Escarpment region.

Travel tips:
Autumn is the best time to visit for colorful foliage.
Reservations are required for some routes during peak times.
Wear sturdy shoes when hiking on rocky terrain.

Pukaskwa National Park: Rugged wilderness along Lake Superior

Why it's a must:
Pukaskwa offers a true wilderness experience on the shores of Lake Superior with dramatic cliffs, dense coniferous forests and pristine beaches.

Top attractions and activities:
Coastal Trail: A challenging multi-day hike with incredible lake views.

White River Suspension Bridge: A scenic bridge that spans the rushing waters below.
Camping & Stargazing: Enjoy the dark skies and peaceful surroundings at remote campsites.

Wildlife Watching: Look for bald eagles, elk and black bears.
Travel tips:
Be prepared for remote conditions with limited cell service.
Pack layers as the weather can change quickly near the lake.
Bring binoculars for bird watching along the coast.

Ontario's natural wonders offer endless opportunities for outdoor adventure, whether you're paddling through tranquil lakes, hiking rugged cliffs or exploring vast forests. Each region has unique landscapes and experiences and is a paradise for nature lovers.

Pro Tips for Exploring Ontario's Natural Wonders:
Always check park websites for seasonal closures and trail conditions.
When hiking, take essentials such as a map, a first aid kit and plenty of water.
Respect wildlife and practice Leave No Trace principles to preserve Ontario's natural beauty.

Historical and cultural sites throughout the province

Ontario is a treasure trove of cultural and historical landmarks that provide a deep insight into its rich past and vibrant present. From world-class museums to Indigenous heritage sites, travelers can explore a variety of attractions that tell the story of Ontario's diverse heritage.

Must-visit museums and heritage sites

Ontario has a variety of museums and historical attractions that provide insight into the province's development, from its early indigenous roots to its colonial past and modern cultural diversity.

Royal Ontario Museum (ROM) – Toronto

One of Canada's largest and most comprehensive museums, featuring art, culture and natural history exhibitions from around the world.

Highlights include indigenous artifacts, dinosaur fossils and ancient Egyptian relics.

The First Peoples Gallery showcases the history and contributions of Indigenous communities in Ontario.

Tips for visitors:

Visit us on Fridays after 5:00 p.m. and receive reduced admission.

Allow at least 3-4 hours to explore the main exhibits.

Canadian History Museum – Ottawa

Located across the river in Gatineau, this museum explores the social and cultural history of Canada.
The Great Hall features impressive totem poles and aboriginal architectural styles.
Interactive exhibits about early settlers, modern immigration and war history.

Tips for visitors:
Combine your visit with a stroll along the Ottawa River and enjoy scenic views of Parliament Hill.
Book guided tours to gain deeper insights into the exhibitions.

Fort Henry National Historic Site – Kingston

Why visit:
A UNESCO World Heritage Site that offers a glimpse into 19th century military life.
Offers live reenactments, military parades and tours.
Panoramic views of the St. Lawrence River and Lake Ontario.

Tips for visitors:
Visit us in the summer months to witness the famous sunset ceremonies.
Consider a night tour for an atmospheric historical experience.

Casa Loma - Toronto

Why visit:

A large European-style castle in the heart of Toronto. Offers a glimpse into early 20th century aristocratic life with secret passages and beautifully preserved rooms. Seasonal events such as the Legends of Horror haunted experience.

Tips for visitors:
Arrive early to avoid crowds, especially on weekends.
Use the audio guides to learn more about the history of the castle.

A must for indigenous cultural sites
Ontario is home to many Indigenous communities and travelers can explore places that showcase their rich heritage, traditions and contributions to the province's cultural fabric.

Woodland Cultural Center – Brantford
Former site of the Mohawk Institute Residential School, now a museum that teaches visitors about Native history and the residential school system.
Offers exhibits on Haudenosaunee culture and art.
Cultural workshops and events take place here all year round.

Tips for visitors:
Work with Indigenous leaders to better understand the impact of residential schools.
Respect the importance of the website and pay attention to sensitive topics.

Petroglyphs Provincial Park – Near Peterborough

It is home to Canada's largest collection of Indigenous rock art, estimated to be over 1,000 years old.

Known as "The Teaching Rocks" with depictions of animals, people and spiritual symbols.

Includes a visitor center that offers insight into the spiritual meaning of the carvings.

Tips for visitors:

Photographing the petroglyphs is not permitted out of respect for their sacred nature.

Visit us during off-peak hours for a quieter experience.

Manitoulin Island – The Heart of Indigenous Culture

The largest freshwater island in the world offers a deep insight into Anishinaabe culture and traditions.

Cultural experiences include powwows, storytelling sessions and art galleries.

Attractions include the Great Spirit Circle Trail and the Ojibwe Cultural Foundation.

Tips for visitors:

Plan a visit around the annual Wikwemikong Cultural Festival for a complete experience.

Participate in guided cultural experiences offered by indigenous communities.

Killarney Provincial Park – Indigenous connection to the land

Stunning landscapes linked to the traditions and history of the Anishinaabe people.
Learn about the Indigenous connection to the park with guided walks and interpretive programs.
Ideal for those interested in hiking, canoeing and learning more about Indigenous stewardship of the land.

Tips for visitors:
Book guided tours to gain insights into indigenous ecological knowledge.
Respect the natural environment and follow conservation guidelines.

Historic towns and villages worth exploring
In addition to major cities, Ontario is home to many small, historic towns that provide insight into the province's beginnings and cultural development.

Niagara-on-the-Lake
Known for its well-preserved 19th century architecture and charming ambience.
Attractions include Fort George, historical walking tours and the Shaw Festival Theater.
Tip: Stroll along Queen Street with its quaint shops and historic inns.

St. Jacobs
Home to Ontario's thriving Mennonite community, offering insights into the traditional rural way of life.
Features a busy farmers market, artisan shops, and horse-drawn carriage rides.

Tip: Visit us during the annual St. Jacobs Sparkle Festival for a festive experience.

Stratford

Famous for the Stratford Festival, celebrating Shakespeare and classical plays.
The historic downtown offers beautiful architecture and artistic cafes.
Tip: Book festival tickets in advance during the summer season.

Ontario's cultural and historical sites offer travelers the opportunity to learn about the province's diverse heritage, from indigenous traditions to colonial history to modern multicultural influences. Whether you're visiting world-famous museums or discovering hidden heritage treasures, there's something for every history and culture lover.

Chapter 8:

Exploring Ontario's Cities

Toronto: The living metropolis

Ontario is home to vibrant cities that offer a mix of history, culture and modern attractions. From the bustling metropolis of Toronto to the historic charm of Ottawa to the quaint small towns full of character, Ontario's urban centers have something to offer every traveler.

Toronto: The Heart of Ontario

Toronto, Canada's largest city, is a dynamic metropolis known for its cultural diversity, iconic skyline and vibrant neighborhoods.
Whether you're interested in world-class attractions, diverse culinary experiences or hidden gems, Toronto offers an unforgettable experience.

Main attractions in Toronto

CN-Turm
One of the tallest free-standing structures in the world.
Offers panoramic views from the observation deck and EdgeWalk adventures.

Tip: Visit the place at sunset for the best views and fewer crowds.

Royal Ontario Museum (ROM)

An extensive collection of exhibits from the areas of art, culture and natural history.

Perfect for families and history buffs.

Ripleys Aquarium of Canada

An underwater adventure with thousands of marine species.

Tip: Buy tickets online to avoid long queues.

Distillery District

A pedestrian street with 19th-century architecture, art galleries, and craft breweries.

Tip: Visit the Christmas market in winter.

Toronto Islands

A short ferry ride from downtown offers a tranquil retreat with beaches and outdoor activities.

Tip: Rent a bike to explore the entire island efficiently.

The best neighborhoods to explore in Toronto

Downtown Core: The business center with top attractions like the Eaton Center and Nathan Phillips Square.

Kensington Market: An artsy district with vintage shops, street art and various restaurants.

Yorkville: High-end boutiques, art galleries and luxury hotels.

The Beaches: A relaxed lakefront neighborhood ideal for a stroll along the promenade.

Unique experiences in Toronto

Catch a Toronto Raptors or Blue Jays game at the Scotiabank Arena/Rogers Centre.

Enjoy a multicultural culinary tour and sample cuisines from Chinatown, Little Italy, and Greektown.

Explore the street art scene in Graffiti Alley.

Ottawa: Canada's capital

Ottawa, the country's capital, is rich in history, government landmarks and cultural institutions. It offers a perfect mix of historic charm and modern vibrancy.

The most important historical sites and government landmarks

Parliament Hill

Famous Gothic-style government buildings overlooking the Ottawa River.

Tip: Watch the Changing of the Guard ceremony in summer.

Rideau Canal

A UNESCO World Heritage Site that becomes the largest ice skating rink in the world in winter.

Tip: Rent a canoe in summer to enjoy the scenic views.

National Gallery of Canada

Home to an extensive collection of Canadian and Indigenous art.

Tip: Don't miss the famous "Maman" spider sculpture in front of the gallery.

Canadian History Museum

Located across the river in Gatineau, the museum offers a fascinating glimpse into Canada's past.

Tip: Plan a visit at the same time as temporary exhibitions.

ByWard Market

A historic farmers market with restaurants, shops and nightlife.

Tip: Try the famous BeaverTail pastries here.

Ottawa's best neighborhoods to explore

The Glebe: Trendy shops, cafes and Lansdowne Park for events and sport.

Centretown: Bustling with government offices, great restaurants and cultural venues.

Hintonburg: A hip neighborhood known for craft breweries and local art galleries.

Unique experiences in Ottawa

In winter you can explore the Rideau Canal by boat or go ice skating.

Explore the political heart of Canada on a guided parliamentary tour.

Attend events like Winterlude, celebrating winter culture and ice sculptures.

Smaller cities and towns: Kingston, London, Thunder Bay

Smaller towns with big character

While Toronto and Ottawa offer big-city attractions, Ontario's smaller cities offer charm, rich history and unique experiences.

Niagara-on-the-Lake

A picturesque city known for its wineries, historic sites and scenic beauty.

Top attractions:

Fort George National Historic Site: A Glimpse of the War of 1812.

Niagara Wine Region: Visit renowned vineyards and enjoy wine tasting.

Shaw Festival: A renowned theater festival celebrating plays by George Bernard Shaw and others.

Tips:

Rent a bike to explore the vineyards at your own pace.

Visit in spring or fall to enjoy fewer crowds and picturesque scenery.

Stratford

A cultural hotspot known for its Shakespearean heritage and artistic atmosphere.

Top attractions:

Stratford Festival: World-famous for high-quality theater productions, including Shakespeare classics.

Avon River: A beautiful place to walk and watch swans.

Local Boutiques: Unique shops selling crafts, antiques and specialty goods.

Tips:

Book theater tickets in advance as shows sell out quickly.

Enjoy farm-to-table food at local restaurants.

Kingston

Ontario's first capital city, rich in history and waterfront beauty.

Top attractions:
Fort Henry: A living history museum showcasing 19th century military life.
1000 Islands Cruise: Explore the stunning islands and scenic views.
Queen’s University: One of Canada’s oldest and most picturesque campuses.

Tips:
Take a ghost tour to learn about Kingston's eerie past.
Visit the waterfront and enjoy the beautiful sunset views.

Collingwood

A charming town known for its proximity to the Blue Mountains and outdoor adventures.

Top attractions:
Blue Mountain Resort: Skiing in the winter, hiking and ziplining in the summer.
Scenic Caves Nature Adventures: Suspension bridge with breathtaking views.
Georgian Bay Beaches: Perfect for water activities and relaxation.

Tips:
Visit in the fall to enjoy lush vegetation and fewer tourists.
Book spa experiences at nearby resorts for a relaxing vacation.

Ontario's cities and towns offer diverse experiences for all types of travelers. Whether you're looking for exciting city life, historical exploration, or small-town charm, Ontario has it all.

Chapter 9:

A culinary journey through Ontario

Signature dishes and local specialties

Ontario's culinary scene is a delicious blend of traditional Canadian flavors, multicultural influences and locally sourced ingredients. From iconic comfort foods to globally inspired dishes, Ontario offers a rich dining experience that caters to every palate.

Traditional dishes to try in Ontario

Ontario's traditional cuisine reflects its cultural diversity and agricultural wealth. Travelers should not miss these typical dishes that define the food culture of the province.

Pea flour and bacon sandwich

Often referred to as "Toronto's signature sandwich," this dish consists of cured pork loin rolled in cornmeal and served in a soft bun.
Where to try: Toronto's St. Lawrence Market is famous for the best peameal bacon sandwiches.
Tip: Enjoy with mustard and pickles for an authentic taste.

Butter tarts

A classic Canadian pastry consisting of a flaky crust filled with a sweet, gooey mixture of butter, sugar and eggs.
Where to try it: Bakeries in small towns across Ontario, particularly in the Kawarthas region.
Tip: Try variations with raisins or pecans for extra flavor.

BeaverTails

A deep-fried, hand-spread pastry in the shape of a beaver tail, topped with cinnamon sugar, chocolate or maple syrup.
Where to try: Popular at festivals, events and places like ByWard Market in Ottawa.
Tip: The classic cinnamon-sugar topping is a must, but adventurous flavors like Nutella or cheesecake are also popular.

Tourtière

A savory meat pie made from ground pork, beef, and spices, often enjoyed during the holidays.
Where to try: French-Canadian restaurants in Ottawa and throughout Eastern Ontario.
Tip: Pair with homemade cranberry sauce for a traditional experience.

Poutine

Originally from Quebec but popular throughout Ontario, poutine consists of crispy French fries topped with cheese curds and smothered in gravy.
Where to try it: Restaurants, pubs and food trucks across Ontario, with variations like pulled pork or truffle sauce.

Tip: Try a gourmet version at poutine specialty shops for unique toppings.

Ontario corn on the cob

Sweet, buttery corn grown on Ontario's farmland and particularly popular in the summer.
Where to try it: Farmers markets and roadside stands in rural areas.
Tip: Enjoy it grilled with a touch of butter and salt for a simple but delicious treat.

Maple syrup delicacies

Ontario is known for its high-quality maple syrup, used in everything from pancakes to baked goods.
Where to try it: Sugar shacks in regions like Muskoka and Lanark County during maple syrup season.
Tip: Visit in the spring to witness the syrup making process and taste fresh maple taffy.

Fish specialties from the lake

Ontario's lakes offer fresh catch such as walleye, trout and bass, often served grilled or fried.
Where to try: Lakeside restaurants in Muskoka, Kingston and the Kawarthas.
Tip: For an authentic experience, order it pan-fried with local, seasonal vegetables.

Ontario cheese

The province is home to numerous artisanal cheesemakers, offering varieties such as aged cheddar, brie and blue cheese.

Where to try: Local markets and specialty cheese shops, with Prince Edward County being a cheese lover's paradise.
Tip: Combine Ontario cheese with local wines for a perfect taste experience.

Nanaimo-Riegel
A no-bake dessert with layers of chocolate, custard and coconut crumbs.
Where to try it: Bakeries across Ontario, with variations like peanut butter or mint flavor.
Tip: Enjoy with a cup of locally roasted coffee for a sweet treat.

Ontario's culinary landscape offers travelers the opportunity to enjoy traditional flavors while exploring the province's vibrant food culture. Whether you indulge in a classic pea and bacon sandwich or savor the sweetness of butter tarts, there's a delicious experience waiting around every corner.

Pro Tips for Foodies:
Visit local farmers markets to purchase fresh, seasonal ingredients.
Take a food tour in cities like Toronto or Ottawa to discover hidden culinary gems.
Look for farm-to-table restaurants that feature Ontario's best local produce.

Best Restaurants, Farmers Markets and Food Tours

Exploring Ontario's vibrant food scene goes beyond restaurants – local markets, guided food tours and unique dining experiences offer travelers the opportunity to connect with the province's culinary heritage in unforgettable ways.

The Best Local Markets in Ontario

Ontario's markets are a foodie's paradise, offering fresh produce and artisan crafts and a chance to experience local food culture first-hand.

St. Lawrence Market (Toronto)

A historic market with fresh produce, meats, cheeses and specialty foods. It is an iconic foodie destination in Toronto.
Must try: peameal bacon sandwich, fresh bagels and local cheese.
Tip: Arrive early to avoid the crowds and enjoy samples from the vendors.

ByWard Market (Ottawa)

One of Canada's oldest public markets featuring local produce, gourmet treats and handcrafted goods.
Must try: BeaverTails, handmade chocolate and fresh maple products.
Tip: Explore nearby cafes and bakeries for authentic local flavors.

Hamilton Farmers Market (Hamilton)

A diverse selection of fresh products, international delicacies and baked goods.
Must try: Fresh bread, sausages and homemade jams.
Tip: Find out about seasonal events and live cooking demonstrations.

Kitchener Market (Kitchener-Waterloo)
Known for its strong European influence, particularly German-style food and delicacies.
Must try: sausages, schnitzel and locally roasted coffee.
Tip: Visit us during the Oktoberfest season and enjoy special culinary offers.

St. Jacobs Farmers' Market (Region Waterloo)
Canada's largest year-round farmers market with a focus on Mennonite and farm-fresh produce.
Must try: Homemade cakes, fresh produce and maple syrup.
Tip: Experience the rural surroundings on a horse-drawn carriage ride.

Kensington Market (Toronto)
A multicultural center with eclectic shops, food stalls and street vendors offering international flavors.
Must-try: empanadas, Jamaican patties and vegan treats.
Tip: Stroll through the colorful streets and discover unique food finds.

The Best Food Tours in Ontario

Food tours offer a guided experience of Ontario's diverse culinary scene, offering insight from local experts while indulging in the region's best flavors.

Culinary Adventure Co. (Toronto, Ottawa)
Offers comprehensive culinary tours featuring multicultural cuisines, hidden gems and historical insights.
Highlight tour: “Kensington Market International Food Tour” with tasting of various dishes from around the world.

Niagara-on-the-Lake Wine and Food Tours
Explore Ontario's famous wine country and enjoy fine dining at local vineyards and restaurants.
Highlight tour: “Winery & Gourmet Pairing Tour” with locally produced wines and artisan cheeses.

Culinary walking tours through Ottawa
Why Join: Discover Ottawa's rich culinary history with tours focused on the ByWard Market and the Rideau Canal area.
Highlight tour: Taste of ByWard Market with local specialties like BeaverTails and gourmet poutine.

Stratford Chocolate Trail (Stratford)
A self-guided tour of decadent chocolate experiences from local chocolatiers and cafes.
Highlight Tour: Visit local chocolate shops to purchase truffles, brownies and sip chocolate.

Muskoka Craft Beer Tours
A must for beer lovers looking to sample Ontario's best craft breweries in the scenic Muskoka region.
Highlight Tour: "Brewery and Distillery Tour" with tastings of craft beer, cider and spirits.

Unique Ontario dining experiences
Ontario offers a range of unique dining experiences for adventurous foodies and those seeking something special.

Canoe (Toronto)
A dining experience with breathtaking views of the Toronto skyline and a menu of Canadian-inspired dishes.
Must-try: Ontario lamb, arctic char and seasonal tasting menus.
Tip: Reserve a window seat for the best sunset views.

360 Restaurant im CN Tower (Toronto)
Enjoy changing panoramic views of Toronto while indulging in a locally inspired menu.
Must-try: Ontario beef, Niagara wines and maple-infused desserts.
Tip: Your dining experience includes access to the tower's observation deck.

Langdon Hall Country House Hotel & Spa (Cambridge)

A luxurious dining experience in a historic property with farm-to-table cuisine using ingredients from the on-site gardens.
Must try: tasting menus with seasonal, regional products.
Tip: Combine your meal with a relaxing stay in the elegant hotel.

The Elora Mill (Elora)
A beautifully restored mill overlooking the Grand River offering fine farm-to-table cuisine.
Must try: Locally inspired dishes made with ingredients from surrounding farms.
Tip: Enjoy a walk through Elora Gorge before or after your meal.

The Lake House (Vineland)
A lakefront dining experience in the Niagara region, known for its romantic ambience and fresh seafood.
Must-try: Freshly caught lake fish and Ontario-grown vegetables.
Tip: Ideal for a romantic dinner with a wonderful lake view.

Borealis Grille & Bar (Guelph/Kitchener)
The focus is on serving 100% Ontario grown and raised food in a casual, eco-friendly atmosphere.
Must-try: Ontario grass-fed beef burgers and locally brewed craft beers.
Tip: Check out the seasonal menu for limited-time offers.

Elchfabrik (Toronto)
A rustic Canadian-style steakhouse offering hearty dishes in a cozy atmosphere.
Must-try: Prime rib and traditional Canadian-style poutine.
Tip: A great place to experience authentic Canadian hospitality.

Fogo Island Fish (Toronto Pop-Up)
An exclusive pop-up experience featuring sustainable seafood flown in from Fogo Island in Newfoundland.
Must try: Cod fish and chips with traditional Newfoundland spices.
Tip: Follow social media for location updates.

Ontario's culinary landscape is as diverse as its people, offering something for every traveler. Whether you stroll through a bustling market, take a food tour or treat yourself to a dining experience, Ontario offers unforgettable gastronomic adventures.

Pro Tips for Foodies:
Book food tours in advance, especially during peak tourist seasons.
Explore local markets early in the morning to buy the freshest produce.
Try seasonal specialties for an authentic experience.

Craft breweries and wineries to visit

Home to some of Canada's best wineries and craft breweries, Ontario offers exceptional taste experiences in picturesque landscapes. Whether you're exploring the famous Niagara wine region or discovering hidden craft beer gems in urban centers, there's something for every beverage lover.

The Best Ontario Wineries to Visit

Weingut Peller Estates (Niagara-on-the-Lake)
A premier winery offering award-winning wines, comprehensive tours and a luxurious dining experience.

Must try: Ice wine, Cabernet Franc and Chardonnay.
Experience tip: Try the unique 10Below Ice Wine Lounge, where tastings take place in sub-zero temperatures.

Inniskillin-Weine (Niagara-on-the-Lake)
Famous for the groundbreaking Canadian ice wine, offering in-depth tastings and vineyard tours.

Must try: Vidal ice wine and Riesling.
Experience tip: Book an ice wine and food pairing for a gourmet experience.

Weingut Jackson-Triggs (Niagara-on-the-Lake)
A modern winery known for its innovative winemaking techniques and summer concert series.

Must try: Sauvignon Blanc, Pinot Noir and sparkling wines.
Experience tip: Enjoy the open-air amphitheater events with wine and live music.

Stratus Vineyards (Niagara-on-the-Lake)
A sustainable, gravity-flow winery producing premium blends with a focus on environmental responsibility.

Must try: Stratus Red and White blends.
Experience tip: Take a guided tour of the vineyards to learn more about their environmentally friendly practices.

Colio Estate Wines (Lake Erie North Shore)
One of Ontario's oldest wineries, offering an enchanting getaway with beautifully aged wines.

Must try: Chardonnay and Merlot.
Experience tip: Visit us in the fall for grape harvest events and grape stomping activities.

Prince Edward County Wineries
Prince Edward County is a rising star in Ontario's wine scene, known for its cool-climate wines and scenic countryside. Top wineries include:
Closson Chase Vineyards – Must try: Chardonnay and Pinot Noir.
Hinterland Wine Company – Must try: sparkling wines.
Norman Hardie Winery – Must try: Gamay and Riesling.

Experience tip: Go on a wine bike tour through the region's picturesque routes.

Weingut Trius (Niagara-on-the-Lake)
A mix of classic and modern wine experiences, known for its bold red wine blends.
Must try: Trius red, rosé and sparkling wines.
Experience Tip: Try the Wine and Food Tasting Flight and enjoy a pairing of wine and chef-prepared appetizers.

The best craft breweries to visit in Ontario
Ontario has a thriving craft beer scene, offering everything from crisp lagers to experimental ales brewed with local ingredients.

Muskoka Brewery (Bracebridge)
A pioneer in Ontario's craft beer scene, located in the scenic Muskoka region.
Must try: Mad Tom IPA and Cream Ale.
Experience tip: Take a brewery tour and enjoy the atmosphere on the lakeshore.

Steam Whistle Brewing (Toronto)
Housed in a historic train engine shed, it offers crisp, refreshing Pilsners.
Must try: Steam Whistle Pilsner.
Experience tip: Enjoy a brewery tour with a look behind the scenes of the traditional brewing process.

Flying Monkeys Craft Brewery (Barrie)

Known for its creative, bold beer styles and vibrant branding.
Must try: Hoptical Illusion IPA and Chocolate Manifesto Stout.
Experience tip: Visit the brewery's taproom for experimental seasonal beers.

Beau's All Natural Brewing Co. (Vankleek Hill)
A family-run organic craft brewery with a commitment to sustainability.
Must try: Lug Tread Lagered Ale.
Experience tip: Try the seasonal offerings, which are prepared with locally sourced ingredients.

Mill Street Brewery (Toronto)
A leader in Toronto's craft beer scene with a variety of traditional and innovative brews.
Must try: organic lager and tankhouse ale.
Experience tip: Visit the original brewpub in Toronto's historic Distillery District.

Collective Arts Brewing (Hamilton)
A unique brewery that combines craft beer with art, with labels designed by international artists.
Must try: Life in the Clouds IPA and Ransack the Universe IPA.
Experience tip: Check out the art exhibitions and beer pairing events.

Amsterdam Brewery (Toronto)

An established brewery with water views and a selection of craft classics.
Must try: Boneshaker IPA and 3 Speed Lager.
Experience tip: Enjoy a beer flight and relax on the BrewHouse terrace.

Great Lakes Brauerei (Etobicoke)
A pioneer of the craft beer industry in Ontario, known for producing small batch beers.
Must try: Canuck Pale Ale and Octopus want to combat IPA.
Experience Tip: Visit the retail store to snag limited releases.

Cowbell Brewing Co. (Blyth)
A state-of-the-art brewery offering farm-to-glass experiences in a charming rural setting.
Must try: Absent Landlord Kolsch and Hazy Days IPA.
Experience tip: Enjoy a tour of their brewery and sustainability initiatives.

Tips for visiting Ontario's wineries and breweries
Book in advance: Many wineries and breweries require reservations, especially on weekends and during peak season.
Designated driver or tour: Consider taking a guided tour or hiring a driver if you plan to visit multiple locations in one day.

Pair it with local food: Enrich your experience by sampling wine and beer pairings with local cheeses, meats and produce.
Visit during off-peak hours: Early mornings or weekdays have a more relaxed atmosphere with personalized attention from staff.
Take home a souvenir: Many locations offer exclusive releases or limited-edition bottles that make great gifts or keepsakes.

Ontario's wineries and craft breweries offer an incredible opportunity to sample the region's flavors while enjoying scenic views and warm hospitality. Whether you're indulging in a glass of Niagara ice wine or sipping a cold IPA at a lakeside brewery, Ontario's beverage culture offers something for everyone.

Pro Tip: Don’t forget to look for special tasting events and wine/beer festivals happening year-round!

Chapter 10:

Shopping and souvenirs

Traditional markets and craft shops

Ontario offers a diverse shopping experience, from bustling urban shopping districts to charming markets full of local crafts and souvenirs. Whether you're looking for high-end brands, unique artisan products or iconic Canadian memorabilia, the province has something to offer every shopper.

Popular shopping streets and districts

Queen Street West (Toronto)

Considered one of Toronto's hottest shopping districts, Queen Street West offers a mix of boutiques, vintage shops and international brands.

What to buy: Indie fashion, handmade jewelry, local artwork.

Tip: Head west from Spadina Avenue to find a mix of major retailers and unique designer boutiques.

Yorkdale Mall (Toronto)

One of Canada's most luxurious shopping centers with world-class fashion, international brands and flagship stores.

What to buy: Designer clothes, high-tech gadgets, premium beauty products.

Tip: Visit on weekdays to avoid crowds and take advantage of the personal shopping service.

Eaton Center (Toronto)
A popular downtown shopping destination with over 250 stores ranging from mainstream to high-end brands.

What to buy: Fashion, electronics, Canadian souvenirs.
Tip: Use the underground PATH system to connect to nearby attractions and avoid winter weather.

ByWard Market (Ottawa)
A historic market area with a mix of local boutiques, craft stalls and unique souvenirs.

What to buy: Arts and crafts, Canadian maple syrup, indigenous art.
Tip: Explore the place in the morning for a quieter shopping experience and fresh local produce.

St. Lawrence Market (Toronto)
A historic market known for its local food vendors, specialty foods and handmade items.
What to buy: Artisan cheeses, fresh produce, Canadian smoked meats.
Tip: Look out for the famous Peameal Bacon Sandwich – a must-try snack while shopping.

Das Rideau Center (Ottawa)

A large shopping complex with major international brands and Canadian retailers.

What to buy: Trendy fashion, cosmetics and luxury accessories.
Tip: The Rideau Center is conveniently located near Parliament Hill, making it easy to combine shopping and sightseeing.

Der Distillery District (Toronto)
A pedestrian street full of boutiques, art galleries and unique shops in historic Victorian-era buildings.
What to buy: Handcrafted spirits, local artwork, stylish interiors.
Tip: Visit us during the Christmas market for festive shopping experiences.

Blue Mountain Village (Collingwood)
A charming mountain resort village with unique boutiques and outdoor gear shops.
What to buy: Ski and hiking gear, handmade pottery, cozy winter clothing.

Tip: Check out local art galleries that feature Ontario artists.

Shopping districts and malls in major cities

Indigenous arts and crafts

Ontario has a rich Indigenous heritage and visitors can find authentic artwork and handcrafted crafts at the following locations:
Woodland Cultural Center (Brantford) – Authentic First Nations artwork and traditional crafts.
Petroglyphs Provincial Park (Woodview) – Indigenous art inspired by ancient rock carvings.
What to buy: Dream catchers, hand-carved wooden sculptures, traditional beadwork.
Tip: Look for authenticity tags to ensure items were actually made by Indigenous artists.

Canadian maple syrup and treats
No trip to Ontario is complete without bringing home legendary maple syrup or sweet treats. Top spots include:
Sugarbush Maple Syrup Festival (Vaughan and Halton Hills) – Seasonal events featuring fresh syrup and maple candy.
St. Jacobs Farmers' Market (Waterloo Region) – Large selection of maple products from local farmers.
What to buy: Maple syrup, maple butter and maple-infused chocolate.
Tip: Opt for Grade A syrup for the best quality and flavor.

Handcrafted ceramics and pottery
Ontario has a thriving artisan community that produces beautiful pottery and ceramics.
Kingston Pottery Market (Kingston) – Handcrafted kitchenware and decorative ceramics.

Elora Center for the Arts (Elora) – Presents the work of local ceramic artists.
What to buy: Handcrafted mugs, decorative plates, artistic sculptures.
Tip: Consider purchasing one-of-a-kind pieces directly from artists at local craft fairs.

Group of seven art prints

The legendary Group of Seven painters have captured Ontario's natural beauty in their works, making their prints a popular souvenir.

Art Gallery of Ontario (Toronto) – Extensive collection of Group of Seven reproductions.
Muskoka Arts & Crafts Fair (Muskoka) – Find local artists for style inspiration.
What to buy: Framed prints, art books, postcards.
Tip: Choose a print that features Ontario landscapes, such as Algonquin Park or Georgian Bay.

Local clothing and accessories

Ontario-based designers offer unique fashion pieces and accessories that make great souvenirs.
Roots Canada (multiple locations) – Iconic Canadian brand offering stylish and comfortable clothing.
Hudson's Bay (nationwide) – Home of the famous HBC strip products.
What to buy: Winter coats, plaid shirts, HBC blankets.
Tip: Look for labels made in Canada for authentic local designs.

Specialty foods

Bring a taste of Ontario home with specialty foods and locally produced goods.

Prince Edward County (PEC) – Famous for artisan cheeses and fine wines.

Niagara Region – Home to unique jams, honey and artisan preserves.

What to buy: Ice wine, cheddar cheese, local fruit preserves.

Tip: Many farmers markets offer shipping options if you don't want to transport items.

Souvenirs with a local touch

Looking for unusual and regionally specific gifts? Consider items that highlight Ontario's character, such as:

Moose-themed souvenirs – available at tourist shops in Northern Ontario.

Toronto Raptors and Maple Leafs fan merchandise – ideal for sports fans.

Handmade soap and candles - using local ingredients such as lavender and beeswax.

Tip: Gift shops in areas like Niagara Falls and the CN Tower offer a wide selection of Ontario-themed gifts.

Tips for Shopping in Ontario

Tax Considerations: Ontario has a 13% HST (Harmonized Sales Tax) which may be added to your purchases. Some tourist shops offer visitors a tax refund.

Haggling: Haggling is not common in retail stores, but may be possible at outdoor markets or craft fairs.

Payment methods: Credit and debit cards are widely accepted, but with smaller providers it makes sense to have some cash with you.
Eco-Friendly Shopping: Bring reusable bags as many stores charge for plastic bags.

There's something for everyone when shopping in Ontario, from luxury fashion and high-tech gadgets to unique crafts and delicious local treats. Whether you're strolling through upscale Toronto malls or exploring charming small-town artisan markets, you're sure to find the perfect souvenir of your visit.

Pro tip: Take the time to explore different areas and support local artisans to find truly unique finds.

Unique Ontario souvenirs to take home

Ontario offers a variety of distinctive souvenirs that reflect its rich culture, natural beauty and diverse heritage. Whether you're looking for locally made goods, delicious treats, or Indigenous artwork, here are some must-have souvenirs to take home from your Ontario trip.

Indigenous crafts

Ontario is home to many indigenous communities and their traditional crafts make a meaningful souvenir. Seek:

Handcrafted Beaded Jewelry: Intricate necklaces, bracelets and earrings made by indigenous artisans.
Dream Catchers: They symbolize protection and good dreams and are widely used in indigenous shops.
Birchbark Canoe Miniatures: Beautifully crafted replicas depicting Ontario's early Indigenous forms of transportation.
Handmade Moccasins: Moccasins made of soft leather decorated with bead embroidery, a unique and practical souvenir.

Sources of supply:
Woodland Cultural Center (Brantford)
Native Canadian Centre von Toronto
Craft shops on Manitoulin Island
Tip: Shop from authentic, indigenous shops to support the local community.

Maple syrup product
Ontario is famous for its high-quality maple syrup, harvested from the province's sugar maple trees. Consider taking home the following:
Pure maple syrup: Packaged in decorative bottles shaped like maple leaves.
Maple sugar candies: Sweet treats made from 100% maple sap.
Maple Butter: A rich, spreadable treat perfect for pancakes or toast.
Maple-Infused Whiskey: A unique Ontario liqueur with a smooth, sweet taste.

Sources of supply:
St. Lawrence Market (Toronto)
Sugarbush farms across Ontario
Specialty stores in Niagara-on-the-Lake
Tip: Look for Grade A syrup for the best quality.

Canadian ice wine

Ontario, particularly the Niagara Region, is known worldwide for its exceptional ice wine. This sweet, concentrated dessert wine makes a luxurious gift. Choose from:

Classic Vidal ice wine – Rich and fruity, perfect for pairing with desserts.

Cabernet Franc Ice Wine – A red variety with berry and spice notes.

Sparkling Ice Wine – A sparkling twist on the traditional dessert wine.

Sources of supply:
Niagara wineries such as Inniskillin and Peller Estates
LCBO (Liquor Control Board of Ontario) stores.
Duty-Free-Shops am Toronto Pearson International Airport
Tip: Pack ice wine carefully so it doesn't break during travel.

Ontario style clothing

Show your love for Ontario with stylish and practical clothing souvenirs, such as:

Roots Canada Hoodies: A classic Canadian brand known for its cozy, high-quality sweatshirts.

"Toronto" or "Canada" T-shirts: Available at gift shops and boutiques.
Check Flannel Shirts: A Canadian-style classic perfect for outdoor adventures.
Hockey Jerseys: Represent Ontario's NHL teams such as the Toronto Maple Leafs or Ottawa Senators.

Sources of supply:
Roots stores across Ontario
CF Toronto Eaton Centre
Souvenir shops in tourist areas
Tip: Look for limited edition designs featuring local landmarks.

Locally made chocolate and snacks
Ontario is home to several artisan chocolate makers and snack makers offering delicious treats such as:
Kawartha Dairy Ice Cream (Take-Home Packs): Iconic Ontario ice cream available in unique flavors.
Soma Chocolate: Handcrafted bean-to-bar chocolate with unique flavors like wild blueberries and birch syrup.
Ontario Honey: Sourced from local farms, ideal for tea or cooking.
Butter Tart: A classic Canadian dessert, available fresh or packaged.

Sources of supply:
Local farmers markets
Specialty food stores like Soma Chocolatemaker
Duty free shops at the airport

Tip: Check the authenticity of products marked "Made in Ontario."

Books about Ontario

As a meaningful souvenir, consider taking home books that depict Ontario's history, culture or nature, such as:
Travel Guide: Featuring hiking trails, hidden gems and city highlights.

Indigenous Storybooks: Traditional stories passed down through generations.
Photo Books: Stunning images of Ontario's landscapes and wildlife.

Sources of supply:
Indigo Bookstores
Souvenir shops in the museum
Local independent bookstores
Tip: Look for books by Ontario-based authors to gain authentic insights.

Handcrafted pottery and artwork

Ontario has a thriving artisan community offering unique handcrafted ceramics and artwork including:
Muskoka Inspired Ceramics: Inspired by Ontario's cottage country.
Group of seven art prints: Famous Canadian landscape artists depicting the beauty of Ontario.
Hand-blown glass pieces: Beautiful and delicate works from local glassblowing studios.

Sources of supply:
Distillery District in Toronto
Ontario Craft Council Galleries
Craft shops in Muskoka and Niagara
Tip: Inquire about shipping options for fragile items.

Hockey memorabilia

As the birthplace of hockey culture in Canada, Ontario offers a wide range of hockey souvenirs such as:
Toronto Maple Leafs merchandise: jerseys, pucks and signed memorabilia.
Hockey Hall of Fame Collectibles: Unique items celebrating the history of the sport.
Vintage Hockey Poster: Featuring legendary players and iconic moments.

Sources of supply:
Hockey Hall of Fame Gift Shop (Toronto)
Official NHL stores
Sporting goods stores across Ontario
Tip: Hockey gear makes a great gift for sports fans.

Natural beauty products

Bring a piece of Ontario's natural surroundings home with locally made beauty products such as:
Prince Edward County Lavender Products: Soaps, Lotions and Essential Oils.
Ontario Beeswax Candles: Eco-friendly, long-lasting and scented with natural oils.
Algonquin Park-inspired skincare: products made with natural ingredients sourced from Ontario's forests.

Sources of supply:
Local markets and wellness shops
Lavendelfarmen im Prince Edward County
Craft shops in cottage country
Tip: Look for organic and cruelty-free labels.

Canoe-themed souvenirs

Ontario's lakes and rivers make canoeing an iconic activity. Souvenirs related to this tradition include:
Miniature Wooden Canoes: Handcrafted replicas perfect for display.
Canoe Paddle: Decorated with Indigenous art or Ontario landscapes.
Canoe-themed clothing: hats and shirts with iconic designs.

Sources of supply:
Country-style souvenir shops
Outdoor and adventure stores such as MEC (Mountain Equipment Co-op)
Indigenous cultural centers
Tip: Choose lightweight items to make packing easier.

Ontario offers a wide range of souvenirs that capture its spirit and culture. Whether you're interested in Indigenous art, gourmet food or iconic Canadian memorabilia, there's something for every traveler to take home as a treasured memory.

Pro Tip: Buy locally made items to support small businesses and artisans while maintaining authenticity.

Chapter 11:

Planning travel routes

One-day highlights in Toronto or Ottawa

Planning a trip to Ontario can be an exciting but overwhelming task, given the province's vast size and diverse attractions. Whether you're here for a few days or a longer stay, a well-thought-out itinerary can help maximize your experience. In this chapter, we present itinerary suggestions based on trip length and travel style to ensure every traveler gets the most out of their visit.

Three-day itineraries for balanced exploration

3-Day Ontario Highlights Itinerary (Ideal for First-Time Visitors or Weekend Travelers)
Tag 1 – Toronto Exploration:
Visit the CN Tower and enjoy panoramic views of the city.
Explore the Royal Ontario Museum (ROM) and nearby Queen's Park.
Stroll through the Distillery District, known for its historic charm and artisan shops.
Enjoy dinner at the St. Lawrence Market and sample local specialties.

Tag 2 – Day trip to Niagara Falls:

Take an early morning drive or bus to Niagara Falls (1.5 hour drive from Toronto).
Experience the Hornblower Cruise and see the falls up close.
Explore Clifton Hill and its attractions.
In the afternoon, visit a Niagara winery for a tasting.
In the evening you return to Toronto.

Tag 3 – Cultural and natural attractions:
Start your day at Kensington Market, a hub for multicultural cuisine and street art.
Take a relaxing stroll along the Toronto Islands and enjoy views of the city skyline.
End your trip with a visit to the Art Gallery of Ontario (AGO) before departure.

Week-long adventures in key regions

7-Day Ontario Adventure Tour (Ideal for travelers looking for a mix of city and nature)
Tag 1-2 – Toronto and Niagara Falls:
Follow the three-day itinerary above for a great city and nature experience.

Tag 3 – Kingston & Thousand Islands:
Head to Kingston for a 1000 Islands cruise exploring the scenic waterways.
Visit Fort Henry, a national historic site that showcases military heritage.
Stay in Kingston and explore the local food scene.

Tag 4-5 – Ottawa Exploration:
Visit the famous Parliament Hill and watch the Changing of the Guard ceremony.
Discover Canada's history at the Canadian Museum of History.
Stroll along the Rideau Canal, a UNESCO World Heritage Site.
Enjoy the bustling shops and restaurants of ByWard Market.

Day 6-7 – Algonquin Park Adventure:
Travel to Algonquin Provincial Park for hiking, canoeing, and wildlife viewing.
Stay overnight in a cozy cabin or at a campsite.
Explore the park's scenic hiking trails and lakes before heading back to town.

14-Day Ultimate Ontario Tour (for travelers who want to immerse themselves in the province's culture and landscapes)
Take 1-4 – Toronto and Niagara Region:
Follow the three-day itinerary and add a day to explore Casa Loma, High Park and the lively Harbourfront Centre.

Take 5-7 – Ottawa & Gatineau Park:
Extend your stay in Ottawa with a visit to the Canadian War Museum.
Head to Gatineau Park for hiking and scenic drives.

Take 8-10 – Muskoka & Algonquin Park:
Experience Ontario's cottage country with a relaxing stay in Muskoka, known for its pristine lakes and luxury resorts.
Canoeing, hiking and stargazing in Algonquin Provincial Park.

Take 11-14 – Exploring Northern Ontario:
Travel to Sudbury, home of the famous Science North Museum.
Visit Manitoulin Island, the largest freshwater island in the world, rich in indigenous culture and nature.
End your trip with a scenic drive along the north shore of Lake Superior, stopping in charming small towns.

Travel plans for different types of travelers

For families with children
Ideal duration: 5-7 days
Main Destinations: Toronto, Niagara Falls, Blue Mountain Resort
Recommended activities:
Ripley's Aquarium of Canada: Interactive exhibits for children.
Ontario Science Centre: Hands-on learning experiences.
LEGOLAND Discovery Center: A fun indoor activity in Vaughan.
Niagara Butterfly Conservatory: A magical experience for young children.

Blue Mountain Resort: Family-friendly adventure activities year-round.

Tips:
Opt for family-friendly hotels with amenities like pools and breakfast options.
Consider attraction passes to save money.

For solo travelers
Ideal duration: 3-10 days
Main destinations: Toronto, Ottawa, Kingston, Algonquin Park
Recommended activities:
Take a solo walking tour of Toronto's diverse neighborhoods.
Enjoy the vibrant nightlife and meet locals in the entertainment districts.
Try adventure activities like canoeing in Algonquin Park.
Discover cultural attractions such as the National Gallery of Canada.
Take a scenic train ride through rural Ontario.

Tips:
Use ride-sharing apps to easily navigate cities.
Join group tours to meet other travelers.

For adventure seekers

Ideal duration: 7-14 days
Main destinations: Algonquin Park, Bruce Peninsula, Muskoka, Thunder Bay

Recommended activities:
Go canoeing and camping in Algonquin Provincial Park.
Hike the Bruce Trail, Canada's oldest and longest marked trail.
Try winter sports at Blue Mountain and Horseshoe Resort.
Visit Kakabeka Falls, known as the “Niagara of the North.”
Explore caves and cliffs in Bruce Peninsula National Park.

Tips:
Rent camping gear from local outfitters for outdoor adventures.
Always check weather conditions before planning outdoor activities.

For history and culture lovers
Ideal duration: 5-10 days
Main destinations: Toronto, Ottawa, Kingston, Niagara-on-the-Lake
Recommended activities:
Tour the Royal Ontario Museum and Casa Loma in Toronto.
Experience Ottawa's Rideau Canal, a UNESCO World Heritage Site.
Explore Fort York and learn about Ontario's colonial past.
Visit historic wineries in Niagara-on-the-Lake.
Take a cultural tour of indigenous sites like Petroglyphs Provincial Park.

Tips:
Consider booking tours for deeper historical insights.
Plan visits during heritage festivals for immersive experiences.

No matter what type of traveler you are or how much time you have, Ontario offers something for everyone. From world-famous landmarks to off-the-beaten-track gems, these suggested itineraries will help you get the most out of your trip while ensuring a memorable and fulfilling experience.

Pro tip: Always check seasonal availability and reserve in advance, especially during peak tourist seasons.

Chapter 12:

Day trips and excursions

Trips to Niagara Falls and Wine Country

The Best Ways to Experience Niagara Falls

Boat tours:

Hornblower Niagara Cruises: Get up close to the falls on this legendary cruise (available April through November).

Jet Boat Tours: Thrilling high-speed rides on the Niagara River, perfect for adventure seekers.

Maid of the Mist (US side): Alternative boat tour for those crossing the border.

Scenic Viewpoints:

Journey Behind the Falls: Explore tunnels behind the cascades for a unique perspective.

Skylon Tower Observation Deck: Panoramic views of the falls and surrounding area from a height of 775 feet.

Niagara Parkway: A scenic drive with multiple overlooks for photography and relaxation.

Helicopter flights:

Niagara Helicopters: Aerial flights offer breathtaking views of the waterfalls, river and nearby vineyards.

Booking tips: Make reservations in advance during peak season to avoid long waits.

Other attractions:

Niagara SkyWheel: A giant Ferris wheel with heated gondolas that offers a bird's-eye view of the falls.

White Water Walk: A boardwalk walk along the mighty rapids of the Niagara River.

Clifton Hill: Entertainment district with attractions such as wax museums and indoor amusement parks.

Top wineries in Niagara-on-the-Lake for tours and tastings

Peller Estates Winery – Known for its ice wine and elegant winery tours.

Inniskillin Wines – A pioneer in Canadian ice wine production with guided tastings.

Jackson-Triggs Winery – Offers vineyard tours and fine dining on site.

Trius Winery – specializes in sparkling wines with curated wine pairing experiences.

Reif Estate Winery – One of Niagara's oldest wineries, known for premium red and white wines.

Stratus Vineyards – Offers sustainable winemaking and boutique tastings.

Pro tips:

Book tastings in advance, especially on weekends.

Consider a guided wine tour to explore multiple wineries without having to worry about driving.

Look for seasonal wine events like vintage festivals and food pairings.

Plan the perfect itinerary for a day trip

Morning:

Arrive early to beat the crowds at Niagara Falls.

Enjoy a boat tour or a scenic overlook.

Stroll the Niagara Parkway and visit Journey Behind the Falls.

Afternoon:

Head to Niagara-on-the-Lake for a wine tour and lunch at a vineyard restaurant.

Explore the charming city center with boutiques and art galleries.

Visit a second winery for an afternoon tasting.

Evening:

Return to Niagara Falls for the nighttime illuminations or fireworks (seasonal).

Dine with a view at Skylon Tower's revolving restaurant.

For entertainment, take a leisurely stroll along Clifton Hill.

Food recommendations:

The Keg Steakhouse & Bar (Fallsview) – Stunning views of the illuminated falls.

Peller Estates Winery Restaurant – Farm-to-table dishes paired with winery wines.

Queenston Heights Restaurant – Overlooking the Niagara River and historic ambience.

Seasonal activities to enjoy

Winter (December–March):

Winter Lights Festival: Thousands of twinkling lights along the Niagara Parkway.

Ice Wine Festival: Sample award-winning ice wines in the snow-capped vineyards.

Frozen Falls View: Experience the partially frozen falls and fewer crowds.

Spring (April–June):

Cherry blossoms in Niagara Parks.

Spring Wine Tours: Discover fresh seasonal releases and food pairings.

Wildlife Viewing: Niagara Glen for bird watching and hiking.

Summer (July–September):

Niagara Grape and Wine Festival.

Fireworks over the Falls: Spectacular displays on summer evenings.

Outdoor Picnics: Enjoy lunch in the vineyard and gatherings in the park.

Autumn (October–November):

Fall colors in Niagara Parks.

Grape harvest tours: insights behind the scenes of the vineyards.

Pumpkin Farms and Markets: Seasonal local produce and events.

Transportation: How to get to Niagara Falls from major cities

From Toronto:

By car: 90-minute drive via Queen Elizabeth Way (QEW); free of charge.

By Bus: GO Transit and FlixBus offer direct service from Union Station.
By Train: VIA Rail offers scenic rides to Niagara Falls Station.
Guided Tours: Numerous day tours with round-trip transportation and attractions included.
From Ottawa:
By Car: Approximately 5.5 hours drive via Highway 401 and QEW.
By Bus: Greyhound and Megabus options with multiple stops.
By Train: VIA Rail offers comfortable service on scenic routes.

Aus Buffalo (USA):
By car: 30-minute drive via Rainbow Bridge border crossing.
By Shuttle: Various cross-border shuttles operate between Buffalo and Niagara Falls in Canada.

Pro tips for getting around:
Consider the WEGO bus system for easy access to Niagara attractions.
Rent bikes to explore the scenic trails along the Niagara Parkway.
Parking near major attractions can be expensive. Therefore, park further away and use the shuttle.

Algonquin Park and Muskoka Escapes

Outdoor activities in Algonquin Park

Algonquin Provincial Park, Ontario's oldest and most famous park, offers a wide range of outdoor activities for nature lovers and adventure seekers:

Hiking trails:

Booth's Rock Trail (3.1 miles): Scenic views of Rock Lake and a historic railroad bed.

View Trail (1.3 miles): A short but steep climb that leads to panoramic views of the park.

Centennial Ridges Trail (10.4 km): Challenging trail with rewarding views of fall foliage.

Spruce Bog Boardwalk (1.5 km): An easy, family-friendly trail ideal for bird watching.

Mizzy Lake Trail (11 km): Excellent for viewing moose, beavers and loons in their natural habitat.

Canoeing and kayaking:

Over 2,400 lakes and a network of rivers offer endless paddling opportunities.

Popular canoe routes:

Canoe Lake: Historic paddling routes with scenic views.

Oxtongue River: Perfect for gentle paddling and exploring waterfalls.

Barron Canyon: Dramatic cliffs and calm waters make it ideal for a day trip.

Canoe rentals are available from several outfitters in and around the park.

Animal observations:

Discover famous Canadian wildlife such as:
Moose, deer and black bears.
Beavers and otters along the waterways.
A wide variety of bird species including loons and ospreys.
Best places for wildlife: Highway 60 Corridor, Mizzy Lake Trail and Hailstorm Creek.
Visit early morning or late evening to enjoy the best sightings.

Fishing:
Algonquin's lakes are rich in trout, bass and pike.
Popular fishing lakes include Lake Opeongo and Cedar Lake.
Permits are required and can be obtained at the park offices.

The best places in Muskoka for relaxation and staycations
Muskoka is a top destination for those seeking lakeside relaxation, cozy cabin accommodations and luxurious resorts.

Top-Resorts am See:
JW Marriott The Rosseau Muskoka Resort & Spa: Upscale resort with lake views and fine dining.
Deerhurst Resort: Family-friendly resort with activities like golf, spa and adventure sports.
Taboo Muskoka Resort & Golf: Perfect for couples looking for a romantic getaway with scenic golf courses.

Trillium Resort & Spa: Rustic charm combined with wellness retreats.

Charming Cabin Stays:

Muskoka Lakes Cottages: Private waterfront cottages for a peaceful retreat.

Port Cunnington Lodge: Historic lodge with stunning views of the Lake of Bays.

Bonnie Lake Resort: Offers cozy cottages in a tranquil forest setting.

Relaxation and Activities in Muskoka:

Boat Trips: Experience the scenic lakes on a classic Muskoka steamboat.

Spa Retreats: Many resorts offer spa services with lake views.

Hiking Trails: The Hardy Lake Provincial Park Trail is perfect for a scenic walk.

Sunset Kayaking: Rent a kayak for a quiet paddle at dusk.

Packaging for outdoor trips

When exploring Algonquin or Muskoka, travelers should pack wisely for an enjoyable experience:

Clothing:

Layered clothing for fluctuating temperatures.

Waterproof jacket and sturdy hiking boots.

Quick-drying clothing for paddling activities.

Warm layers for fall and winter visits.

Walk:

Lightweight backpack for day hikes.

Binoculars for animal observation.
Waterproof map or GPS device for canoe routes.
Bug spray (especially in the summer months).
Headlamp or flashlight for evening trips.

Food and supplies:
High-energy snacks like trail mix and protein bars.
Reusable water bottles or hydration packs.
First aid kit with essentials such as bandages and antiseptic wipes.
Bear-proof containers for food storage at campsites.

Tips for camping vs. staying overnight in lodges

Camping in Algonquin:
Choose between camping in the foothills (accessible by car) or in the hinterland (by canoe).
Popular backcountry locations: Pog Lake, Mew Lake and Canisbay Lake.
Backcountry camping requires permits and careful planning.
Follow Leave No Trace principles to protect nature.
Reservations should be made in advance, especially in high season.
Stay overnight in lodges:
Lodges offer more comfort with amenities such as meals, guided tours and cozy cabins.
Killarney Lodge and Arowhon Pines are popular locations in the park.
Lodges are ideal for those who prefer a mix of nature and comfort.

Choose between the two:

Camping is best for adventure seekers who want to enjoy a rugged experience.

Lodges are suitable for families and couples seeking relaxation with modern amenities.

Some lodges offer hybrid options that combine rustic cabins with dining options.

Best time to travel for seasonal activities

Autumn (September to October):

Peak season for stunning fall foliage with vibrant reds, oranges and yellows.

Best places for fall colors: Lookout Trail, Ragged Falls and Muskoka's Maple Trail.

Ideal for hiking, photography and sightseeing.

Winter (December to March):

Perfect for snowshoeing, cross-country skiing and winter camping.

Popular ski resorts: Deerhurst Resort and Hidden Valley Resort.

Look out for frozen waterfalls and snow-covered landscapes.

Visit winter festivals like the Muskoka Winter Carnival.

Spring (April to June):

Best for wildlife viewing when animals emerge after winter.

Enjoy fewer crowds and mild weather.

Spring blossoms and fresh greenery provide excellent hiking conditions.

Summer (July to August):
Ideal for canoeing, kayaking and swimming in the lakes.
Long daylight hours allow for extended outdoor adventures.
Perfect for family trips, with campfire evenings and water sports.
Attend events such as the Muskoka Arts & Crafts Show and Canada Day celebrations.

Pro tips for travelers:
Book accommodation early: it fills up quickly in high season, especially in autumn and summer.
Check Park Regulations: Algonquin has strict rules regarding waste disposal and fire safety.
Beware of bears: Store food properly and remain vigilant in wilderness areas.
Capture the sunrise: Early morning offers the best light for photos and fewer crowds.
Explore off the beaten path: Go beyond Highway 60 to quieter, less touristy areas.

Cultural visits to indigenous communities

Home to a rich Indigenous heritage, Ontario offers travelers unique cultural experiences that provide insights into the traditions, art and way of life of the First Nations, Métis and Inuit. The best cultural experiences include:

Powwows and cultural festivals:

Experience traditional dancing, drumming and regalia at annual powwows where indigenous communities celebrate their culture and heritage.
Grand River Champion of Champions Powwow (Six Nations) – A vibrant presentation of music, dance and indigenous craftsmanship.
Curve Lake First Nation Powwow – A family-friendly event featuring traditional songs and ceremonies.
Manitoulin Island Powwow Trail – A summer event series featuring several First Nations communities.

Heritage centers and cultural sites:
Woodland Cultural Center (Brantford): A museum dedicated to the history and culture of the Haudenosaunee peoples, featuring educational exhibits and the history of residential schools.
Petroglyphs Provincial Park: Home to the largest collection of Indigenous rock carvings in Canada depicting spiritual beliefs and daily life.
Ojibwe Cultural Foundation (Manitoulin Island): Offers workshops, storytelling, and exhibitions on Ojibwe arts and traditions.
Sainte-Marie among the Hurons (Midland): A reconstructed 17th-century Huron-Wendat village that offers deep insights into traditional life.

Guided tours and practical experiences:
Many indigenous communities offer tours that provide an authentic insight into their history and contemporary life:

Great Spirit Circle Trail (Manitoulin Island): Guided experiences such as canoe heritage tours and story walks.
Wikwemikong Tourism: Operated by the Wikwemikong Unceded Territory and offers eco-tours and cultural workshops.
Indigenous Experiences (Ottawa): Traditional music, food and craft demonstrations on Victoria Island.

Recommended Indigenous Destinations in Ontario

Manitoulin Island:
The largest freshwater island in the world is rich in indigenous culture. Several First Nations communities offer cultural tourism experiences.
Visitors can explore the Great Spirit Circle Trail, participate in cultural workshops, and visit sacred sites such as the Cup and Saucer Trail, which offers breathtaking views of the island.
Seasonal powwows and storytelling events provide insight into Anishinaabe traditions.

Six Nations of the Grand River:
The largest First Nations reserve in Canada, home to the Haudenosaunee (Iroquois) people.
Highlights include the Woodland Cultural Center, Chiefswood National Historic Site (birthplace of poet E. Pauline Johnson), and unique artisan shops selling handmade beadwork and moccasins.

Experience the annual Champion of Champions Powwow or take a guided cultural tour.

Curve Lake First Nation (near Peterborough):
A vibrant community known for its rich powwow traditions and authentic Indigenous art.
Visit the Whetung Ojibwa Centre, which features an extensive collection of First Nations art, jewelry and crafts.

Fort William Historical Park (Thunder Bay):
A living history site showcasing the culture and contributions of the Anishinaabe people, including traditional canoe building demonstrations and fur trade reenactments.
Tips for treating indigenous traditions and communities respectfully
When visiting indigenous communities, it is important to approach cultures sensitively and respectfully.

Important tips:
Get permission: Always ask before taking photos, especially during ceremonies or in sacred areas.
Participate in events respectfully: Powwows and ceremonies have specific protocols in place: listen to announcements, dress modestly, and stand during the flag and honor singing.
Support Local Businesses: Buy authentic Indigenous products directly from artisans and businesses to support the community.

Use appropriate language: Learn and use respectful terminology when referring to Indigenous peoples and their cultural practices.
Participate Wisely: Participate in cultural experiences with genuine interest and openness, avoiding stereotypes or assumptions.

Authentic Indigenous cuisine and where to find it

Ontario offers a variety of opportunities to sample traditional Indigenous cuisine, which includes locally sourced ingredients such as wild rice, game meat and berries.

Popular Indigenous Dishes to Try:

Bannock: A traditional bread often served with jam, honey or as a side dish to stews.
Three Sisters Soup: Made with corn, beans and squash, a dish rooted in indigenous agricultural traditions.
Deer Stew: A hearty meal made with locally sourced game meat.
Wild rice dishes: Often mixed with mushrooms, cranberries or maple syrup.
Fry Bread Tacos: A modern twist on traditional ingredients.

Where to Find Authentic Indigenous Food:

Kūkŭm Kitchen (Toronto): Specializes in indigenous fusion cuisine and features dishes like bison burgers and arctic char.

Pow Wow Café (Toronto): Famous for its Indigenous-inspired fried bread tacos and seasonal dishes.
Cedar Spoon Indigenous Catering (Ottawa): Offers traditional Anishinaabe dishes for special occasions.
Feast Café Bistro (Thunder Bay): Serves dishes made from fresh, locally sourced ingredients with an indigenous culinary influence.

Cultural souvenirs to take home
Visitors can take home meaningful souvenirs that support Indigenous artisans and celebrate Ontario's cultural diversity.

Popular souvenirs you should consider:
Handmade beadwork: earrings, necklaces and bracelets with traditional patterns and colors.
Dream Catcher: A symbolic and beautifully crafted item that originates from the Ojibwe culture.
Canoes and artifacts made from birch bark: small replicas of traditional craftsmanship.
Indigenous Artwork: Paintings, carvings and prints depicting spiritual and cultural themes.
Incense Kits: Contains sage, sweetgrass and cedar used in traditional ceremonies.
Books and Storytelling Materials: Written by Indigenous authors to learn about their heritage and legends.

Where to buy authentic indigenous goods:
Whetung Ojibwa Center (Curve Lake First Nation): Extensive collection of arts and crafts.

Woodland Cultural Center Gift Shop (Brantford): Authentic crafts and books.
Toronto and Ottawa Indigenous Markets: Regular markets featuring Indigenous artisans.
Indigenous-owned online stores: Support artisans directly through websites that promote ethical, handcrafted products.

Pro tips for travelers:
Respect sacred spaces: Do not enter forbidden areas without permission.
Plan ahead: Many cultural centers and tours require advance reservations.
Work with local guides: They offer authentic insights and stories not found in guidebooks.
Participate in cultural experiences: Hands-on activities such as drum circles or traditional cooking classes enrich your understanding of indigenous culture.
Be a responsible visitor: Support indigenous communities by contributing to the local economy and learning about their cultural contributions.

Chapter 13:

Entertainment and nightlife

Live music and performing arts venues

Ontario offers a vibrant music scene with venues catering to all genres, from intimate indie concerts to large-scale concerts featuring global superstars. The most famous music venues include:

Toronto:

Massey Hall: A historic concert hall known for its world-class acoustics and home to legendary artists of all genres, from rock to classical.

Scotiabank Arena: The preferred venue for major international concerts featuring top artists such as Taylor Swift, Drake and U2.

Budweiser Stage: A popular outdoor waterfront venue ideal for summer concerts with scenic views of Lake Ontario.

The Danforth Music Hall: A mid-sized venue known for indie and alternative music performances, offering an intimate but energetic atmosphere.

Horseshoe Tavern: A legendary small venue that once hosted major artists like the Rolling Stones and The Tragically Hip.

Ottawa:

Canadian Tire Centre: International tours and major music festivals take place here throughout the year.

National Arts Center (NAC): Offers a mix of orchestral performances, jazz and contemporary music.
Bronson Center Music Theater: An independent venue showcasing local and national talent.
Hamilton:
FirstOntario Centre: A large venue for major touring acts and music festivals.
The Casbah: A cozy venue with live performances from up-and-coming indie artists.
Bridgeworks: A newer venue offering an eclectic mix of music, comedy and community events.
London:
Budweiser Gardens: A multi-purpose arena that hosts everything from rock concerts to orchestral performances.
Aeolian Hall: A historic venue with excellent acoustics, ideal for classical and folk music.
Kingston:
The Grand Theater: A charming venue that hosts concerts and performing arts events with a local touch.

Best cities for theater performances and cultural shows

Ontario's theater scene is world-renowned, offering everything from Shakespearean classics to Broadway-style productions and avant-garde performances.

Important theater goals:

Stratford:

Stratford Festival: One of the world's most famous Shakespeare festivals, showcasing both traditional and modern plays with top-class talent.
Tom Patterson Theater: A newly renovated venue offering innovative productions in an intimate setting.

Toronto:
Mirvish Productions: The leading theater company presenting Broadway hits such as The Phantom of the Opera, Hamilton and Les Misérables at venues including the Princess of Wales Theater and the Royal Alexandra Theatre.
Soulpepper Theater Company: A staple for Canadian and international theater with a focus on classic and contemporary storytelling.
Toronto Fringe Festival: An annual event featuring innovative performances by emerging artists across a variety of genres.

Niagara-on-the-Lake:
Shaw Festival: A world-class theater festival celebrating the works of George Bernard Shaw and contemporary productions, held in a picturesque town known for its wineries and charm.
Ottawa:
National Arts Center (NAC): Presents Canadian and international productions in English and French, including theatre, dance and musical performances.

Tips for theater goers:

Book early: Popular productions, particularly at Stratford and Mirvish venues, sell out quickly.
Matinee performances: These often have lower ticket prices and fewer crowds.
Discount options: Check at the box office for discounts for students, seniors and groups or express same-day tickets.

Tips for finding last minute tickets and special discounts

Whether you want to attend a concert or a theater performance on short notice, here are some strategies for finding cheap tickets:
Online ticket platforms: Sites like Ticketmaster, StubHub, and SeatGeek often offer discounted resale tickets closer to show dates.
Rush and Lottery Tickets: Many theaters offer same-day rush tickets at discounted prices, especially for students and seniors.
Offers at the Box Office: Purchasing locally can sometimes avoid additional service fees and provide better seating options.
Social Media Alerts: Follow venues and production companies on platforms like Twitter and Instagram to receive flash sales or promo codes.
Apps for deals: Download apps like TodayTix to get exclusive deals on theater tickets in cities like Toronto.
Hotel Concierge Service: Upscale hotels often partner with local venues to give guests exclusive access to tickets.

Experience local indie music scenes in Ontario

Ontario is a hotbed of emerging talent, with thriving indie music scenes in cities like Toronto, Hamilton and Ottawa. Travelers can explore local music culture through:

Toronto Indie Scene:

Visit Queen Street West, known for its thriving indie music scene and eclectic venues such as:

The Garrison: Featuring up-and-coming alternative and experimental acts.

Rivoli: Hosts a mix of live music, comedy and spoken word events.

The Cameron House: A center for singer-songwriters and folk artists.

Hamilton Indie Scene:

Hamilton has a strong reputation for supporting rock and folk musicians and features popular venues such as:

This Ain't Hollywood: A local favorite for punk and rock shows.

The Casbah: Presenting indie, folk and blues artists in an intimate setting.

Supercrawl Festival: An annual arts and music festival that highlights indie bands.

Ottawa Indie-Szene:

Ottawa's ByWard Market and surrounding areas offer intimate venues such as:

Live on Elgin: A small venue that features live indie music performances.

The Rainbow Bistro: Known for jazz, blues and indie acts.
CityFolk Festival: Each year features a mix of indie, folk and roots artists.

Tips for discovering indie music in Ontario:
Check local listings: Websites like NOW Toronto and Eventbrite often list upcoming performances and shows at small venues.
Explore music festivals: Indie-friendly festivals like NXNE (North by Northeast) in Toronto showcase new and emerging artists.
Visit vinyl stores and cafes: Record stores like Rotate This and Sonic Boom often host performances or event flyers promoting underground shows.
Exploring Social Media: Follow local bands and artists to stay up to date on pop-up gigs and secret shows.

Pro Tips for Enjoying Live Entertainment in Ontario:
For smaller venues, arrive early to ensure good seating or standing room.
Many venues have age restrictions. Check policies when traveling with younger visitors.
Consider using public transportation to avoid parking issues when attending large concerts.
Follow health and safety guidelines as some venues may have COVID-19 guidelines in place.
Dress comfortably but appropriately for upscale theaters or casual live music venues.

Bars, clubs and entertainment districts

Ontario offers a vibrant music scene with venues catering to all genres, from intimate indie concerts to large-scale concerts featuring global superstars. The most famous music venues include:

Toronto:

Massey Hall: A historic concert hall known for its world-class acoustics and home to legendary artists of all genres, from rock to classical.

Scotiabank Arena: The preferred venue for major international concerts featuring top artists such as Taylor Swift, Drake and U2.

Budweiser Stage: A popular outdoor waterfront venue ideal for summer concerts with scenic views of Lake Ontario.

The Danforth Music Hall: A mid-sized venue known for indie and alternative music performances, offering an intimate but energetic atmosphere.

Horseshoe Tavern: A legendary small venue that once hosted major artists like the Rolling Stones and The Tragically Hip.

Ottawa:

Canadian Tire Centre: International tours and major music festivals take place here throughout the year.

National Arts Center (NAC): Offers a mix of orchestral performances, jazz and contemporary music.

Bronson Center Music Theater: An independent venue showcasing local and national talent.

Hamilton:
FirstOntario Centre: A large venue for major touring acts and music festivals.
The Kasbah: A cozy space with live performances from up-and-coming indie artists.
Bridgeworks: A newer venue offering an eclectic mix of music, comedy and community events.

London:
Budweiser Gardens: A multi-purpose arena that hosts everything from rock concerts to orchestral performances.
Aeolian Hall: A historic venue with excellent acoustics, ideal for classical and folk music.

Kingston:
The Grand Theater: A charming venue that hosts concerts and performing arts events with a local touch.

Best cities for theater performances and cultural shows
Ontario's theater scene is world-renowned, offering everything from Shakespearean classics to Broadway-style productions and avant-garde performances.

Important theater goals:

Stratford:

Stratford Festival: One of the world's most famous Shakespeare festivals, showcasing both traditional and modern plays with top-class talent.

Tom Patterson Theater: A newly renovated venue offering innovative productions in an intimate setting.

Toronto:

Mirvish Productions: The leading theater company presenting Broadway hits such as The Phantom of the Opera, Hamilton and Les Misérables at venues including the Princess of Wales Theater and the Royal Alexandra Theatre.

Soulpepper Theater Company: A staple for Canadian and international theater with a focus on classic and contemporary storytelling.

Toronto Fringe Festival: An annual event featuring innovative performances by emerging artists across a variety of genres.

Niagara-on-the-Lake:

Shaw Festival: A world-class theater festival celebrating the works of George Bernard Shaw and contemporary productions, held in a picturesque town known for its wineries and charm.

Ottawa:

National Arts Center (NAC): Presents Canadian and international productions in English and French, including theatre, dance and musical performances.

Tips for theater goers:

Book early: Popular productions, particularly at Stratford and Mirvish venues, sell out quickly.

Matinee performances: These often have lower ticket prices and fewer crowds.

Discount options: Check at the box office for discounts for students, seniors and groups or express same-day tickets.

Tips for finding last minute tickets and special discounts

Whether you want to attend a concert or a theater performance on short notice, here are some strategies for finding cheap tickets:

Online ticket platforms: Sites like Ticketmaster, StubHub, and SeatGeek often offer discounted resale tickets closer to show dates.

Rush and Lottery Tickets: Many theaters offer same-day rush tickets at discounted prices, especially for students and seniors.

Offers at the Box Office: Purchasing locally can sometimes avoid additional service fees and provide better seating options.

Social Media Alerts: Follow venues and production companies on platforms like Twitter and Instagram to receive flash sales or promo codes.

Apps for deals: Download apps like TodayTix to get exclusive deals on theater tickets in cities like Toronto.

Hotel concierge service: Upscale hotels often partner with local venues to give guests exclusive access to tickets.

Experience local indie music scenes in Ontario

Ontario is a hotbed of emerging talent, with thriving indie music scenes in cities like Toronto, Hamilton and

Ottawa. Travelers can explore local music culture through:

Toronto Indie Scene:

Visit Queen Street West, known for its thriving indie music scene and eclectic venues such as:

The Garrison: Featuring up-and-coming alternative and experimental acts.

Rivoli: Hosts a mix of live music, comedy and spoken word events.

The Cameron House: A center for singer-songwriters and folk artists.

Hamilton Indie Scene:

Hamilton has a strong reputation for supporting rock and folk musicians and features popular venues such as:

This Ain't Hollywood: A local favorite for punk and rock shows.

The Casbah: Presenting indie, folk and blues artists in an intimate setting.

Supercrawl Festival: An annual arts and music festival that highlights indie bands.

Ottawa Indie-Szene:

Ottawa's ByWard Market and surrounding areas offer intimate venues such as:

Live on Elgin: A small venue that features live indie music performances.

The Rainbow Bistro: Known for jazz, blues and indie acts.

CityFolk Festival: Each year features a mix of indie, folk and roots artists.

Tips for discovering indie music in Ontario:

Check local listings: Websites like NOW Toronto and Eventbrite often list upcoming performances and shows at small venues.
Explore music festivals: Indie-friendly festivals like NXNE (North by Northeast) in Toronto showcase new and emerging artists.
Visit vinyl stores and cafes: Record stores like Rotate This and Sonic Boom often host performances or event flyers promoting underground shows.
Exploring Social Media: Follow local bands and artists to stay up to date on pop-up gigs and secret shows.

Pro Tips for Enjoying Live Entertainment in Ontario:
For smaller venues, arrive early to ensure good seating or standing room.
Many venues have age restrictions. Check policies when traveling with younger visitors.
Consider using public transportation to avoid parking issues when attending large concerts.
Follow health and safety guidelines as some venues may have COVID-19 guidelines in place.
Dress comfortably but appropriately for upscale theaters or casual live music venues.

Seasonal events and local festivals

Home to a rich Indigenous heritage, Ontario offers travelers numerous opportunities to experience First Nations, Métis and Inuit cultures first-hand. From lively powwows to heritage centers to authentic cuisine, exploring Indigenous communities offers a deeper understanding of Ontario's cultural landscape.

Important Indigenous Cultural Experiences in Ontario

Travelers can immerse themselves in Indigenous culture through a variety of experiences, including:

Powwows and cultural festivals:

What to Expect: Powwows are lively gatherings featuring traditional drumming, dancing, storytelling and crafts.

Top-Events:

Grand River Powwow (Six Nations): One of the largest and most important powwows in Ontario, held annually in July.

Akwesasne Powwow: Hosted by the Mohawk community, featuring traditional songs and spectacular dance performances.

Curve Lake First Nation Powwow: A celebration of Anishinaabe culture with interactive activities for visitors.

Tip: Dress modestly, get permission before taking photos, and respect ceremonial spaces.

Heritage centers and museums:

Woodland Cultural Center (Brantford): An important center for preserving the history and culture of the Haudenosaunee people, with exhibits on language, art, and residential school heritage.

Petroglyphs Provincial Park: Home to the largest concentration of Indigenous petroglyphs in Canada, with tours and interpretation centers.
Ojibwe Cultural Foundation (Manitoulin Island): Presenting traditional and contemporary indigenous art, music and workshops.
Sainte-Marie among the Hurons (Midland): A reconstructed 17th-century French Jesuit settlement that highlights early interactions between settlers and the Wendat (Huron) people.

Guided Indigenous Tours:

Great Spirit Circle Trail (Manitoulin Island): Offers guided cultural experiences such as canoeing, storytelling and medicine walks led by local Anishinaabe guides.
Wikwemikong Tourism: Offers cultural immersion experiences including drum-making workshops, visits to sacred sites and guided hikes.
Moccasin Trails Tours (Toronto and Niagara): Educational tours that provide insights into Indigenous history in urban and natural settings.

Recommended Indigenous Cultural Destinations

Ontario offers several Indigenous communities where travelers can experience local traditions and customs first-hand:

Manitoulin Island (Nordost-Ontario):

It is known as the largest freshwater island in the world and is home to several First Nations communities.

Visitors can experience this Wiikwemkoong Visit the Unceded Territory, attend cultural festivals and enjoy traditional drum performances.
Key Attractions: Great Spirit Circle Trail, Ojibwe Cultural Foundation and scenic trails with cultural significance.

Six Nations of the Grand River (Southwestern Ontario):
The largest First Nations reserve in Canada with a diverse Haudenosaunee (Iroquois) culture.
Highlights include Chiefswood National Historic Site (home of poet Pauline Johnson) and the annual Grand River Powwow.
The reserve also offers ecotourism experiences and traditional craft workshops.
Curve Lake First Nation (Region Kawarthas):
A great place to explore Anishinaabe culture with attractions such as the Curve Lake Cultural Center and nearby Petroglyphs Provincial Park.
Thunder Bay (Nord-Ontario):
A gateway to learning Anishinaabe traditions, with attractions such as the Anemki Wajiw (Mount McKay) lookout and the Fort William Historical Park, which includes exhibits on Indigenous history.

Tips for treating indigenous traditions and communities respectfully
When visiting indigenous communities, it is important to show respect and cultural sensitivity. Here are some important guidelines:

Do your research: Research the history, traditions and protocols before your visit.
Ask for permission: Always get permission before taking photos, especially during ceremonies.
Respect Sacred Places: Many sites have spiritual significance; Follow the guidelines of local guides.
Support local artisans: Buy authentic indigenous crafts directly from community members instead of mass-produced items.
Participate with an open mind: Be open to learning from an Indigenous perspective without making assumptions.
Use appropriate terminology: Refer to communities by their preferred names (e.g., Anishinaabe, Haudenosaunee, Métis).

Authentic Indigenous cuisine and where to find it

Ontario's Indigenous cuisine combines traditional ingredients such as game, fish, berries and bannock to create delicious dishes that reflect a deep connection to the land. Foods you should definitely try include:

Signature dishes:

Bannock: A traditional flatbread often served with stews or honey.
Three Sisters Soup: A hearty dish made with corn, beans and squash.
Wild Rice: A staple prepared with meat or mushrooms.
Smoked Fish: Common in northern Ontario, particularly around Lake Superior.

Venison and bison: Lean, protein-rich meat traditionally hunted and prepared in indigenous cuisine.

Where to find local cuisine:

Pow Wows and Cultural Festivals: Many events have food stalls serving traditional dishes.

Tea-N-Bannock (Toronto): A cozy spot offering indigenous dishes in an urban setting.

Pow Wow Café (Toronto): Known for its Indian tacos with bannock and traditional toppings.

North American Indigenous Games (various locations): A great opportunity to sample indigenous foods while enjoying sporting events.

Cultural souvenirs to take with you

Supporting Indigenous artists and businesses by purchasing authentic souvenirs is a meaningful way to remember your trip while contributing to the community. Unique souvenirs include:

Handmade items:

Beaded Jewelry: Beautifully intricate earrings, bracelets and necklaces crafted by indigenous artisans.

Dream Catchers: Symbolic items believed to offer protection and positive energy.

Moccasins: Traditional footwear made of soft leather, often decorated with beads.

Carved Totems and Statues: Symbolic Representations of Indigenous Mythology and Heritage.

Birch bark baskets and canoes: Hand-woven or made from natural materials that represent traditional craftsmanship.

Where to buy authentic souvenirs:
Indigenous Shops: Buy directly from galleries like the Woodland Cultural Center Gift Shop or Thunderbird Market (Six Nations).
Festivals and Powwows: A great opportunity to support local artisans selling handmade goods.
Online marketplaces for indigenous peoples: Many communities have official online shops for authentic handicrafts.

By exploring Ontario's Indigenous communities, travelers can gain a deep insight into the region's rich heritage, support local artisans and make meaningful connections.

Chapter 14:

Understanding Ontario's Culture

Indigenous influence and multiculturalism

Ontario's cultural identity is deeply rooted in its Indigenous heritage and is enriched by waves of immigration from around the world. From ancient traditions that still thrive today to a vibrant mix of global influences, Ontario offers travelers a unique cultural experience that blends the old with the new.

Indigenous influence on modern Ontario culture
Indigenous peoples – including the Anishinaabe, Haudenosaunee and Métis – have played a fundamental role in shaping Ontario's identity. Their traditions, values and perspectives continue to influence various aspects of life across the province today.

Cultural contributions that endure:
Language and place names: Many city and landmark names, such as Toronto (derived from the Mohawk word "Tkaronto," meaning "where trees stand in the water"), have indigenous origins.
Environmental stewardship: Indigenous principles of sustainability and respect for the land influence Ontario's conservation efforts, including sustainable tourism and environmentally friendly initiatives.

Arts and Crafts: Indigenous art such as wood carvings, beadwork and paintings remains an important cultural expression in galleries and public spaces.
Traditional Healing Practices: Some health and wellness centers incorporate indigenous healing traditions such as smudging ceremonies and the use of medicinal plants.
Cuisine: Native ingredients such as wild rice, bison and maple syrup are increasingly used in modern Ontario cuisine.

Where to Experience Indigenous Culture in Ontario:

Woodland Cultural Center (Brantford): A leading institution in the preservation of Indigenous art, language and history.
Petroglyphs Provincial Park: Contains ancient petroglyphs considered sacred by indigenous peoples.
Manitoulin Island: Home to thriving indigenous communities offering cultural tours and workshops.
Six Nations of the Grand River: A must-see to learn about Haudenosaunee culture through guided experiences and annual powwows.

Important historical events that shape Ontario's cultural landscape

Ontario's cultural diversity is rooted in centuries-old historical events that have shaped Ontario's identity today.

Important historical milestones:

Pre-Colonial Era: Indigenous communities thrived with well-established trade routes and systems of governance.
European Contact (1600s): French and British explorers established trade and settlements, which had a profound impact on the native people's way of life.
Loyalist Migration (1780s): Thousands of British Loyalists settled in Ontario after the American Revolution, contributing to the province's English heritage.
Post-World War II immigration boom (1940s-1970s): Waves of immigration from Europe, Asia and the Caribbean diversified Ontario's social fabric.
Multiculturalism Act (1971): Canada's commitment to multiculturalism cemented Ontario's reputation as an inclusive and diverse province.

Experience Ontario's multicultural influences

Ontario is one of the most multicultural regions in the world, with diverse communities influencing food, art, festivals and everyday life. Travelers can immerse themselves in a wide range of cultural experiences that reflect the diversity of the province.

Culinary experiences:

Ontario's food scene is a direct reflection of its multicultural population, offering flavors from around the world.
Toronto: Known as one of the most diverse cities in the world, visitors can explore neighborhoods such as Chinatown, Little Italy, Greektown and Kensington Market to enjoy authentic international cuisine.

Ottawa: The city's ByWard Market area offers a mix of international flavors, including Lebanese, Ethiopian and Vietnamese cuisine.
Hamilton: A growing foodie scene that combines Caribbean, South Asian and European influences.

Art and cultural exhibitions:
Art Gallery of Ontario (Toronto): Features Indigenous and international art collections.
Bata Shoe Museum (Toronto): Showcases shoes from around the world and explores their cultural significance.
Ottawa's National Gallery of Canada: Home to an impressive collection of Indigenous art alongside European masterpieces.
Murals and Street Art: Discover vibrant murals in areas like Graffiti Alley (Toronto) that showcase the city's cultural diversity.

Community festivals and events:
Ontario hosts numerous multicultural festivals throughout the year celebrating the traditions and heritage of its diverse population.
Toronto Caribbean Carnival (Caribana): A vibrant celebration of Caribbean culture with parades, music and dancing.
Taste of Little Italy (Toronto): A food festival featuring authentic Italian cuisine and entertainment.
Chinese New Year celebrations (various cities): Featuring dragon dances, food and cultural performances.

Oktoberfest (Kitchener-Waterloo): One of the largest Oktoberfests outside of Germany, celebrating the province's German heritage.

Opportunities to engage respectfully with indigenous heritage

Travelers can enjoy Ontario's indigenous culture while maintaining respect and understanding of the traditions. Here are some important tips:

Research:

Learn about the history, customs and significance of indigenous traditions before attending events or visiting cultural sites.

Support Indigenous Businesses:

Buy authentic crafts, art and products directly from Indigenous artists and businesses rather than commercial sources.

Participate in cultural experiences respectfully:

When attending events such as powwows, follow cultural protocols such as: B. Standing during ceremonial songs and obtaining permission before taking photographs.

Use correct terminology:

Address indigenous peoples by their correct national or community name (e.g., Anishinaabe, Haudenosaunee) rather than using outdated or generalized terms.

Respect sacred spaces:

Some sites, such as burial sites and ceremonial rooms, are sacred and may have visitor guidelines that must be followed.

Listen and learn:
Engage openly with Indigenous leaders and storytellers and honor their experiences and knowledge.

Ontario's rich cultural offering is a blend of ancient Indigenous heritage and the vibrant influences of its multicultural communities. By experiencing the food, art and festivals, travelers can gain a deeper insight into the province's dynamic cultural landscape while showing respect for its traditions.

Art, music and literature scene

Ontario has a thriving cultural landscape and offers visitors a dynamic mix of art, music and literature. Whether exploring world-class museums, attending live music events, or browsing local bookstores, Ontario offers endless opportunities to immerse yourself in your creative spirit.

Must-visit museums and galleries
Ontario is home to an impressive variety of arts institutions, showcasing both Canadian and international talent. From classic masterpieces to contemporary exhibitions, here are some must-visit places:

Toronto:

Art Gallery of Ontario (AGO):

One of Canada's leading art institutions, featuring works by the Group of Seven, Indigenous artists and international masters such as Picasso and Van Gogh.
Tip: Visit the collection galleries on Wednesday evenings and enjoy free entry.

Royal Ontario Museum (ROM):

A mix of art, culture and history with extensive exhibitions of indigenous art, world cultures and contemporary installations.
Must-see: The Indigenous Art and Culture Gallery, highlighting First Nations creativity.

Vaughan:

McMichael Canadian Art Collection:

Located north of Toronto, this gallery specializes in the work of the Group of Seven and Indigenous artists.
Tip: Take a guided tour to learn more about the influence of Canadian landscapes on artists.

Ottawa:

National Gallery of Canada:

Features an outstanding collection of Canadian and Indigenous art as well as renowned international pieces.
Tip: Check out the Contemporary Canadian Artists section for a modern perspective on cultural expression.

Hamilton:

Hamilton Art Gallery:

A hidden gem with Canadian and international art collections including contemporary exhibitions and public sculptures.

Kingston:

Agnes Etherington Art Centre:
Located at Queen's University, it offers a mix of historical and contemporary pieces, including a notable Rembrandt collection.

Prominent Ontario-born authors, musicians and artists
Ontario has been home to some of the most influential figures in art, music and literature. Visitors can explore her works and even see landmarks related to her legacy.
Famous Ontario Authors:
Margaret Atwood (Toronto): Atwood is known worldwide for “The Handmaid’s Tale” and often explores Canadian identity and environmental issues in her works.
Alice Munro (Wingham): The Nobel Prize-winning short story writer captures the essence of small-town Ontario life in her works.
Michael Ondaatje (Toronto): Author of The English Patient, Ondaatje's work often links history and personal identity.
Joseph Boyden (Willowdale): Known for novels that explore Indigenous culture and history, such as Three Day Road.
Famous Ontario Musicians:

Drake (Toronto): A global icon in hip-hop and R&B, his music draws heavily from Toronto culture and landmarks.
The Weeknd (Toronto): Known for blending R&B and pop with a unique style inspired by his childhood in Toronto.
Neil Young (Omemee): A legendary figure in rock and folk music with strong ties to Ontario's landscapes.
Shawn Mendes (Pickering): A pop sensation with roots in the Greater Toronto Area.
Rush (Toronto): The legendary rock band is closely linked to the city's musical heritage.

Famous Ontario Artists:

Tom Thomson: A pioneering artist whose works depicting the Ontario wilderness inspired the Group of Seven.
Lawren Harris: Harris' work is known for his iconic depictions of Canadian landscapes and is exhibited in many Ontario galleries.
Norval Morrisseau: A renowned Indigenous artist whose bold, colorful work tells stories about Anishinaabe culture.

Tips for finding cultural tours and art walks

Ontario's vibrant arts scene is easily explored with guided tours and self-guided walks that offer deeper insights into the region's creative expression.

Top culture and art tours:

Toronto Art Walks: Self-guided tours of neighborhoods like Queen Street West and the Distillery District, featuring contemporary street art and independent galleries.

Ottawa Indigenous Art Tours: Learn about Indigenous influences on public art installations across the city, including Parliament Hill.

Stratford Festival Art Walk: A perfect mix of Shakespeare theater and public art installations around Stratford.

Graffiti Alley (Toronto): A lively section that showcases some of the city's most famous street art and murals.

Hamilton Art Crawl: Monthly art events featuring local galleries, music and street performances in the city's thriving arts district.

Where to book tours:

Art Gallery of Ontario (AGO) Public Tours: Offers themed tours for deeper insights into the collections.

Viator and Airbnb Experiences: Great platforms to find local art walks and cultural experiences.

Ontario Travel Centres: Local offices provide maps and guides to public art installations and galleries.

Best bookstores and libraries to discover local literature

For those looking to delve deeper into Ontario's literary scene, the province offers some of the best bookstores and libraries where visitors can discover local literature and cultural works.

Top bookstores:

Ben McNally Books (Toronto): A beautifully curated independent bookstore known for its selection of Canadian literature.

Type Books (Toronto): Specializing in Canadian authors and art books with a strong focus on local talent.
The Bookshelf (Guelph): A combination bookstore, cafe and cinema offering a unique literary experience.
Queen Books (Toronto): A cozy, independent bookstore with a wide selection of indigenous and multicultural literature.

Important libraries:

Toronto Reference Library: The largest in Canada and offers an extensive collection of books on Ontario history and culture.
Ottawa Public Library: Home to a large collection of historical archives and local literature.
Kitchener Public Library: Offers an extensive collection of books on Ontario's multicultural heritage.

Tips for book lovers:

Look for author events and book signings at independent bookstores.
Attend literary festivals like the Toronto International Festival of Authors for readings and discussions.
Visit university bookstores for academic papers on Ontario history and culture.

Ontario's arts, music and literary scene offers travelers an enriching experience that delves deep into the province's creative soul. Whether exploring galleries, attending concerts or discovering local authors, visitors are sure to be inspired by Ontario's vibrant cultural offerings.

Social norms and etiquette

Understanding Ontario social norms and etiquette can help travelers interact smoothly and respectfully with one another. Whether you're exploring bustling city centers or charming rural communities, knowing local customs enhances the travel experience and encourages positive interactions with locals.

General customs and behaviors travelers should be aware of

Ontario is known for its polite and inclusive culture, characterized by a mix of Indigenous traditions, European heritage and multicultural communities. The most important behaviors to keep in mind include:

Politeness and politeness:

Saying “please,” “thank you,” and “sorry” are common even in smaller interactions.

It is considered polite to keep doors open for others.

People generally respect personal space and expect the same from others.

Queues (queuing):

Whether in shops, public transport stops or event venues, forming an orderly queue is the norm and standing in line is considered rude.

Punctuality:

Punctuality is particularly valued at business meetings and social gatherings.

It is generally acceptable to be 5 to 10 minutes late for informal social events, but earlier for business meetings.

Respect for diversity:

Ontario embraces cultural diversity and it is important to show respect for different customs, languages and religious practices.
Avoid making assumptions about a person's background based on appearance or accent.

How to navigate social interactions in urban and rural Ontario

Interactions may vary depending on whether you are in a big city like Toronto or a small town in rural Ontario. Here are some differences to keep in mind:

In urban areas (Toronto, Ottawa, Hamilton):

Diversity: Cities are very multicultural and people are used to tourists. Requests for directions or help are usually welcome.
Small talk: Although not as common, casual conversations can take place in places like cafes or parks.
Pace of life: Cities are fast-paced; People seem to be in a rush but are still generally polite.
Public transport etiquette: Free seats for seniors, pregnant women and people with disabilities and avoid loud conversations on public transport.

In rural areas (Muskoka, Prince Edward County, Northern Ontario):

Friendliness: People tend to be more open to small talk and may greet strangers with a nod or smile.

Community spirit: Respect for local traditions and customs is important and travelers should avoid disrupting everyday life.

Driving etiquette: Wave or nod to other drivers, especially on country roads.

Tipping culture in restaurants, hotels and transportation

Tipping is a common practice in Ontario and expected in most service industries. Here's a guide to tipping norms:

Restaurants and cafes:

Standard tip rate: 15-20% of the total bill before taxes.

Increased tipping (20-25%) for exceptional service or fine dining.

Some restaurants may offer automatic tipping for larger groups (6+ people).

Hotels:

Bellhop/porter: CAD 2-5 per piece of luggage.

Housekeeping: CAD 2-5 per night, left in room.

Concierge: CAD 5-10 for special requests or bookings.

Transport:

Taxis and rideshare services (Uber, Lyft): 10-15% of the fare.

Airport shuttle driver: CAD 2-5 depending on baggage assistance.

Tour guide:

On guided tours, if the service is excellent, a tip of 10-20% is customary.

Bars and cafes:

In bars and cafes, the tip is around $1 per drink, or 10-15% of the total bill.

Important cultural behavior rules to keep in mind

Of the:

Respect Indigenous culture and land acknowledgments: Many events begin with a land acknowledgment that recognizes Indigenous territories. Listen respectfully and learn about local First Nations communities.

Dress for the weather: Ontario experiences all four seasons, so travelers should check the weather forecast and dress accordingly.

Recycle and follow environmental guidelines: Ontario values sustainability, so be mindful of waste disposal and recycling.

Follow traffic rules carefully: Pedestrians generally have the right of way and walking across the street is discouraged.

Don'ts:

Don't assume everyone speaks French: While French is an official language, English is more commonly spoken in Ontario. French is more prevalent in Ottawa and the eastern parts of the province.

Don't speak loudly in public spaces: Canadians tend to value quiet public spaces, especially on public transportation and in restaurants.

Do not smoke in public places: Smoking is prohibited in most indoor and outdoor public areas, including patios and parks.

Don't discuss controversial topics casually: Avoid sensitive topics such as politics, religion and indigenous issues unless you are having a respectful and informed discussion.

By considering these social norms and etiquette tips, travelers can ensure they have a respectful and enjoyable experience in Ontario.

Chapter 15:

Travel tips and resources

Emergency contacts and useful numbers

Being prepared for essential emergency contacts and services during your trip to Ontario can make a significant difference. Whether you're in a busy city or a remote rural area, having the right information at your fingertips ensures a safe and stress-free experience.

Important phone numbers for travelers
Travelers should have these important numbers saved in their cell phones or written down in case of emergencies:
Emergency services (police, fire department, ambulance):
Dial 911 for immediate assistance in life-threatening situations across Ontario.
Calls to 911 are free from any phone, including cell phones without service.

Non-emergency police assistance:
Toronto Police: +1 416-808-2222
Ottawa Police: +1 613-236-1222
Ontario Provincial Police (OPP) Rural Areas: +1 888-310-1122
Important hospital emergency departments:
Toronto General Hospital: +1 416-340-3111
The Ottawa Hospital: +1 613-722-7000
Mount Sinai Hospital, Toronto: +1 416-596-4200

Consulates and embassies:
US Consulate General (Toronto): +1 416-595-1700
British High Commission (Ottawa): +1 613-237-1530
Australian Consulate (Toronto): +1 416-323-1155
Travelers should check with their respective embassies for current contact information.
Roadside assistance services:
Canadian Automobile Association (CAA): +1 800-222-4357
Ontario Ministry of Transportation: 511 (for road conditions and closures)
Private roadside assistance services through car rental agencies or insurance providers.

Search for emergency services in major cities and remote areas
Ontario has well-equipped emergency services in major urban centers such as Toronto, Ottawa and Hamilton. However, response times may be longer in remote areas, so travelers should plan accordingly.
Big cities:
Hospitals and clinics are readily available and most urban centers have 24-hour emergency rooms.
Pharmacies such as Shoppers Drug Mart and Rexall offer minor health services and medications.
Police stations are centrally located and public transport staff can help in emergencies.

Remote and rural areas:
Cell service may be limited in regions such as Northern Ontario and Algonquin Park. Consider carrying a

satellite phone or GPS tracking device in case of emergencies.

Many smaller communities rely on volunteer firefighters and paramedics, so calling 911 is still the best option for immediate assistance.

Look for signs along highways directing travelers to the nearest medical facilities.

Tips:

Always check nearby hospitals and clinics before heading to rural areas.

Download offline maps and emergency contacts for areas with limited connectivity.

How to effectively use Ontario's 911 system as a visitor

When calling 911, it is important to remain calm and provide the dispatcher with accurate information. Here's what awaits you:

What you should say:

Clearly state the type of emergency (fire department, medical, police).

Include your exact location (roads crossed, landmarks, GPS coordinates if possible).

Stay on the line until you are asked to hang up.

Language services:

Ontario's 911 services can support multiple languages; Travelers can request an interpreter if necessary.

False calls:

Accidental emergency calls should not be abruptly interrupted; Instead, stay on the line and inform the operator that there was an error.

Essential travel insurance tips and recommendations

Travel insurance is essential for visitors to Ontario to cover unexpected medical costs, trip cancellations or lost items. Travelers should note the following:

Types of Coverage You Should Look For:

Health Insurance: Covers emergency hospital visits, prescriptions and doctor consultations.

Trip cancellation and interruption: Protects against last-minute plan changes due to emergencies.

Lost or Stolen Luggage: Covers the cost of replacing luggage and valuables.

Rental car insurance: If you plan to rent a car, check coverage for collisions and liability.

Recommended travel insurance providers:

Manulife travel insurance

Allianz Global Assistance

World Nomads (ideal for adventure travelers)

CAA Travel Insurance

Tips for choosing the right policy:

Check whether your home health insurance covers international travel.

Choose insurance coverage with 24/7 emergency services.

Have a digital and hard copy of your insurance policy available.

Make sure any planned adventure activities such as skiing, hiking or water sports are covered.

By staying informed and prepared, travelers can explore Ontario with confidence, knowing they have access to reliable emergency resources if needed.

Eco-friendly travel tips for Ontario

Sustainable travel in Ontario allows visitors to enjoy the natural beauty while minimizing their impact on the environment. From eco-conscious accommodations to responsible waste disposal, there are many ways travelers can help preserve the province's landscapes and communities.

How travelers can reduce their carbon footprint
Ontario offers several opportunities to adopt sustainable travel practices:
Use public transport and eco-friendly travel options:
Take advantage of Ontario's extensive public transportation systems such as GO Transit, TTC (Toronto Transit Commission) and VIA Rail to reduce emissions.
Consider biking or hiking in urban areas and on nature trails. Bike sharing programs like Bike Share Toronto offer convenient options.
Choose hybrid or electric cars from companies like Enterprise and Hertz.
Choose direct flights:

When flying to Ontario, choose direct flights to reduce fuel consumption and offset your carbon footprint through airline programs.

Practice responsible use of energy:

Turn off lights and unplug when leaving hotel rooms or Airbnb accommodations.

Save water by reusing towels and minimizing laundry requests.

Dine sustainably:

Support farm-to-table restaurants that source their ingredients locally and ethically.

Choose plant-based meals to reduce the environmental impact of meat production.

Recommended eco-friendly accommodations and travel practices

Many hotels and lodges across Ontario emphasize sustainability and eco-friendly practices. Consider staying at:

Certified green hotels:

Fairmont Royal York (Toronto): Known for its sustainability efforts, including waste reduction and energy conservation.

The Gladstone House (Toronto): A boutique hotel with a focus on sustainability and community engagement.

Blue Mountain Resort (Collingwood): Implements eco-initiatives such as water conservation and waste reduction.

Eco-lodges and sustainable stays:

The Algonquin Eco-Lodge (Algonquin Park): A solar-powered retreat offering a low-impact wilderness experience.
Northern Edge Algonquin: Focuses on sustainable tourism with eco-friendly accommodations and experiences.
Cedar Grove Lodge (Muskoka): A lakefront lodge that values environmental stewardship.

Tips for sustainable stays:
Look for accommodations with LEED certification or Green Key ratings.
Use refillable toiletries instead of single-use plastic items.
Support accommodations that prioritize local suppliers and environmentally friendly practices.

Where to find recycling and waste disposal services
Ontario has a strong waste management system that promotes recycling and proper disposal practices. Travelers can:

Find recycling bins in cities and parks:
Cities like Toronto and Ottawa have clearly marked bins for paper, plastic and compost waste.
Provincial and national parks such as Algonquin and Bruce Peninsula offer recycling stations at campgrounds and visitor centers.
Carry reusable items:

Bring a reusable water bottle, coffee cup, and shopping bag to reduce waste.
Water refill stations are available in many public places, including airports and city parks.

Responsible disposal of hazardous waste:
Medicines and electronic devices should be disposed of at designated drop-off points in pharmacies and recycling centers.
Check local guidelines for waste disposal at Airbnb rentals and hotels.

Support local sustainability initiatives and companies
Travelers can have a positive impact on Ontario's environment and communities by supporting initiatives that focus on conservation and sustainability.
Ecotourism programs:
Take guided eco-tours in areas like Muskoka and Georgian Bay that emphasize wildlife conservation and minimal environmental impact.
Discover locally-led ecotours that focus on sustainable practices and cultural preservation.
Sustainable shopping and eating:
Shop for locally made, eco-friendly products at markets like St. Lawrence Market in Toronto or ByWard Market in Ottawa.
Choose restaurants that participate in the OceanWise Sustainable Seafood Program.
Volunteer opportunities:

Participate in cleanups along the Great Lakes or volunteer for conservation projects with organizations like Ontario Nature and Nature Conservancy of Canada.

Eco-friendly travel apps to use:

"Too Good To Go" – Helps reduce food waste by connecting travelers with restaurants that offer surplus food at reduced prices.

"iRecycle" – Provides information on recycling locations and services across Ontario.

"EcoHotels" – Guides travelers to sustainable accommodation options worldwide.

By implementing these eco-friendly travel tips, visitors can enjoy Ontario's stunning scenery and vibrant cities while contributing to a more sustainable future.

Map guide for your trip

How to download and use the map of Ontario for easy navigation.

Whether you're exploring Ontario's bustling cities or its stunning natural landscapes, a reliable map is essential for navigation. Below are step-by-step instructions for downloading and using Ontario maps for offline and online access.

Choosing the right Ontario card type

Before downloading, decide which type of map suits your travel needs:

City Maps: Detailed maps of cities like Toronto, Ottawa and Niagara Falls with streets, landmarks and transit routes.

Road Maps: Covers highways, scenic routes, and road trip directions.

Topographic Maps: For hikers and outdoor adventurers, showing elevations, trails and natural landmarks.

Offline digital maps: Downloadable versions for use without Internet access.

Tourist Maps: Highlighting important attractions, restaurants and hotels.

How to download Ontario maps online

Option 1: Google Maps (most convenient for general use)

Google Maps is a versatile tool for online and offline navigation.

Steps to Download Ontario Offline Maps:

1. Open the Google Maps app on your smartphone (available for Android and iOS).
2. Search "Ontario" in the search bar.
3. Tap the three-dot menu (top right) and select "Download offline map".
4. Customize the area to include the regions you want to visit (Toronto, Niagara Falls, etc.).
5. Tap "Download" and wait for the map to be saved to your device.
6. Access the offline map by going to Your Profile > Offline Maps in the Google Maps app.

Using the downloaded map:
You can search for places, get directions, and view points of interest even without an internet connection.
However, real-time traffic updates are not available in offline mode.

Option 2: Official Ontario travel and road maps (for detailed planning)
The Government of Ontario provides official travel maps with detailed road networks, points of interest and transit options.
Steps to download from the official website:
1. Visit the official Ontario tourism website: ontariotravel.net
2. Navigate to the Maps and Publications section.
3. Choose from different categories such as: E.g. street maps, city guides and parking maps.
4. Download the PDF version of the desired map to your device.
5. Print the map for physical use if necessary.

Using the downloaded map:
PDF cards can be opened with apps such as Adobe Acrobat Reader.
Use zoom features to focus on specific areas or points of interest.
Printed versions are useful for long car trips without internet access.

Option 3: Maps.me (Offline-GPS-Navigation)

Maps.me offers highly detailed offline maps with walking, cycling and driving routes.

Steps to Download Ontario Maps:

1. Install the Maps.me app from the App Store or Google Play.
2. Open the app and search for "Ontario."
3. Select Ontario from the search results and tap Download.
4. Wait for the download to complete.

Using the downloaded map:

The map provides offline GPS navigation with detailed walking, cycling and driving routes.
You can pin locations and create custom routes.

Option 4: GPS navigation apps (for drivers)
If you're planning a road trip, GPS apps like Waze, HERE WeGo, or Sygic offer Ontario maps with offline features.

Steps to download:

1. Download your favorite app from the App Store or Google Play.
2. Search for "Ontario" in the app's map storage.
3. Download the map and make sure GPS tracking is enabled.

Using the downloaded map:

Provides real-time traffic updates, speed limits and road conditions.

Some apps also offer voice-guided navigation offline.

Using paper maps (for traditional navigation)
For travelers who prefer physical maps, Ontario visitor centers and tourism offices offer free maps including:
Ontario Visitor Centers: Located in cities and major travel centers.
Bookstores: Purchase detailed street atlases at bookstores such as Indigo and travel supply stores.
Gas Stations: Most gas stations offer road maps for purchase.

Use paper maps effectively:
Mark important routes and destinations with markers.
Fold maps to focus on specific regions.
Use a compass for outdoor adventures.

Tips for using Ontario maps effectively

Activate GPS: Even when you're offline, your phone's GPS can track your location on most downloaded maps.
Update maps regularly: Make sure you download the latest versions before traveling.
Use multiple cards: Combine digital maps with printed versions for backup.
Check data usage: Some apps consume mobile data when used online. Therefore, download maps via WiFi.
Plan your routes: Mark key attractions, restaurants and accommodations in advance.

By following these steps, travelers can confidently explore Ontario using the map best suited to their needs, whether online, offline or in print. Let me know if you need any further help!

Diploma

By the end of this guide, it's clear that Ontario is more than just a destination - it's an experience that unfolds in countless ways. From the iconic Toronto skyline to the peaceful shores of the Muskoka Lakes, from the cultural richness of Indigenous communities to the exhilarating adventures of Algonquin Park, Ontario offers something for every traveler. Whether you're here to explore bustling city centers, take scenic road trips or immerse yourself in the province's diverse cultural landscape, Ontario is a place that promises unforgettable moments and endless discoveries.

Thinking about your Ontario trip

Traveling through Ontario isn't just about checking off famous landmarks or sampling local dishes – it's about engaging with a province that thrives on diversity, natural beauty and a rich cultural heritage. As you stroll through the charming towns, vibrant towns and tranquil countryside, you'll notice the distinct mix of tradition and modernity that defines Ontario's character. Every street corner, every festival and every park tells a story – stories of resilience, innovation and inclusivity.

From the world-famous Niagara Falls to the hidden treasures of the northern wilderness, Ontario invites travelers to slow down, look closer and truly connect with their surroundings. Whether you strolled the historic trails of Ottawa, sampled the multicultural flavors of Toronto's Kensington Market, or hiked the majestic cliffs of the Bruce Peninsula, your journey through Ontario is likely to have left you with treasured memories and a deeper appreciation for its unique nature Leave charm.

Carry Ontario with you

As you prepare to leave Ontario, take more than just souvenirs; They carry the warmth of its people, the flavors of its cuisine and the inspiration from its landscapes. Whether it's the sound of rushing waterfalls, the laughter shared at a local café, or the quiet serenity of a lakeside retreat, Ontario leaves an impression on your heart that lasts well beyond your stay.

Remember to carry forward the lessons you learn - respecting the land and its indigenous heritage, having new cultural experiences and finding joy in the simple moments. Ontario teaches us to appreciate nature, celebrate diversity and always remain open to new adventures.

A few final travel tips

Before you say goodbye, here are a few farewell tips to keep your Ontario experience smooth and enjoyable:

Stay curious: Ontario is constantly evolving, with new attractions, restaurants and experiences constantly emerging. Be open-minded and explore beyond the usual tourist attractions.
Support Local: Whether you dine at a family-run restaurant, purchase Indigenous art or stay at an eco-friendly lodge, supporting local businesses helps preserve Ontario's unique character.
Enjoy the Seasons: Each season offers a different perspective on the beauty of Ontario. Plan a return visit to see the province in a new light - be it the vibrant fall colors, the festive winter wonderlands or the lively summer festivals.
Capture the moments: Document your trip with photos, diaries or even a travel blog. Ontario's landscapes and cultural sites provide endless inspiration for thinking about your travels.

Ontario awaits your return

While this guide offers practical advice and insight to help you navigate Ontario with ease, the true essence of this province lies in the experiences you create. Ontario's beauty, culture and adventure are best discovered first-hand, and you'll discover something new every time you visit. Whether you're coming to Ontario for the first time or planning a return trip, Ontario welcomes you with open arms and endless possibilities.

We hope this guide has been a valuable companion on your journey and has inspired you to see Ontario not just as a destination, but as a place of connection, adventure and wonder.

So as you close this book and embark on your Ontario adventure – be it today, tomorrow or in the future – know that the province will always be there, ready to offer you new discoveries, new friendships and new memories offer.

Have a safe trip and see you again in Ontario!

Printed in Great Britain
by Amazon